Citizen Civilized City

compiled and designed by
Lawrence Kasparowitz

"Never doubt that a small group of thoughtful, committed citizens can change the world.

Indeed, it is the only thing that ever has!"

Margaret Mead, Anthropologist
(used with permission)

"If you don't like the news ....
go out and make some
of your own !!"

Wes "Scoop" Nisker, Newscaster

"Amazing what you can accomplish
when you don't care
who gets the credit."

Harry Truman, President

Editor's Note:

Government is a slow and tedious process. While it often includes citizen and neighborhood involvement, non-governmental, private organizations have created movements and interesting groups which can create positive change in our cities and towns.

This book is a compilation and discussion of the changes contemplated, inspired and completed by the citizens of neighborhoods and/or cities around the world. I am fascinated by the way groups are created and how they influence public decision making. This book merely recognizes them and forwards the description of these groups from their own websites.

Each website has been confirmed to be active. The indexes have been compiled by topic and geographical location.

TOPIC INDEX

TOPIC INDEX

TOPIC INDEX

TOPIC INDEX

TOPIC INDEX

TOPIC INDEX

GEOGRAPHIC INDEX

GEOGRAPHIC INDEX

STATES:

GEOGRAPHIC INDEX

GEOGRAPHIC INDEX

CITIES:

GEOGRAPHIC INDEX

Acadiana Economic Development Council

Location: Louisiana

Website: teamarcadiana.org

The Acadiana Economic Development Council (AEDC) welcomes you to Louisiana and the Acadiana region. Here you will find the location, business climate, economic development resources, workforce, and quality of life necessary to establish and grow your business.

AEDC is a non-profit, 501(c)(3) organization founded by local economic developers and incorporated in 2004. AEDC represents the primary economic development organizations in the Acadiana Parishes (Counties) of Acadia, Evangeline, Iberia, Lafayette, St. Landry, St. Martin, and Vermilion.

Explore our website. Discover Acadiana's diversity and the resources available to existing, expanding and relocating businesses, or request more information at info@teamacadiana.org.

Advocates for Urban Agriculture

Location: Chicago, IL

Website: auachicago.org

Advocates for Urban Agriculture (AUA) is a coalition of organizations and individuals interested in learning about, networking and advocating for urban agriculture in the Chicago area.

The group meets quarterly and maintains an array of working groups dedicated to improving the state of urban agriculture in the city of Chicago, with AUA's Steering Committee acting as its governing body.

Our goal is to make this website a comprehensive hub for projects, activities, information, resources, and opportunities in urban agriculture. As the website grows in tandem with this burgeoning movement, take a look around, and be sure to join as a Member of AUA (free!) if you support what we're doing. We also encourage you to join AUA's Google Group; with over 800 members, it's a great place to connect with Chicago's urban agriculture community.

Aga Khan Development Network

Location: International

Website: akdn.org

The agencies of the Aga Khan Development Network (AKDN) are private, international, non-denominational development organizations. They work to improve the welfare and prospects of people in the developing world, particularly in Asia and Africa, without regard to faith, origin or gender. Its programmes are designed to bring a critical mass of economic, social and cultural activities to bear on a given area.

AKDN projects encompass many of the determinants of the quality of life, including the natural and built environments in both urban and rural areas, food security, health, education, access to financial services and economic opportunity, as well as the cultural areas of traditional music, architecture and art. Some programmes, such as specific research, education and cultural programmes, span both the developed and developing worlds.

The AKDN works in 30 countries around the world. It employs approximately 80,000 people, the majority of whom are based in developing countries.

American Architectural Foundation

Location: Nationwide

Website: archfoundation.org

The American Architectural Foundation (AAF) is dedicated to the vibrant social, economic, and environmental future of cities. In the past decade alone, AAF has worked directly with local leaders through more than 500 city engagements. During this time, AAF has served every major metropolitan region and most second tier cities in the United States.

All told, it has provided design leadership training and technical assistance to hundreds of elected officials, public-private partnerships, education leaders, business leaders, and other key local decision makers in the design process.

These engagements are based on real world challenges and opportunities from the participants' cities, which provide the focus for intensive, collaborative design leadership programs. The overarching goal is to equip these leaders with the knowledge, inspiration, and resources that they need to lead their communities to transformative change through design.
To inform its efforts, AAF leverages its extensive network of city leaders and design innovators.

Architectural League of New York

Location: New York, NY

Website: archleague.org

The mission of the Architectural League is to advance the art of architecture. The League carries out its mission by promoting excellence and innovation, and by fostering community and discussion in an independent forum for creative and intellectual work in architecture, urbanism, and related disciplines.

We present the work and ideas of the world's most interesting and influential architects and designers to New York, national and international audiences, through lectures, exhibitions, publications, and the worldwide web. We identify and encourage talented young architects, through competitions, grants, exhibitions, and publications. We help shape the future of our built environment by stimulating debate and provoking design thinking about the critical issues of our time.

The Architectural League's governing documents, conflict of interest policy, and most recent financial report are available upon request to the League.

ARISE Detroit !

Location: Detroit, MI

Website: arisedetroit.org

ARISE stands for Activating Resources and Inspiring Service and Empowerment.

Our goal is to promote a greater citizen involvement and community awareness of organizations and services that help a community function better.

We are creating a permanent network of organizations and their volunteers offering programs that support children and families.

Our mission is to inspire a community of active engagement, personal responsibility and hope by connecting people to opportunities and resources to transform the quality of life for all Detroiters.

Our vision of Detroit is a city where children are loved and mentored, families are healthy and strong, and everyone is instilled with a spirit of hope and engaged in community service.

Art Everywhere US

Location: Nationwide

Website: arteverywhereus.org

Our mission is to provide holistic educational experiences that inspire youth and adults to realize their creative potential in all aspects of life. We encourage their resolve to become active participants in the creation of a spiritually, environmentally and socially sustainable world, strengthening their ability to transform themselves and their communities.

Art Everywhere is a non-profit 501(c)(3).

Take a look at our various services and programs, learn about how Art Everywhere started, discover the people behind the Art Everywhere, find related organizations, and help further our work.

The Soul Ecology project offers participants the opportunity to live, work, learn and play together for a three-week period. The program incorporates elements of theater, ecological building and journaling to further creativity and self-development. The Soul Ecology project includes the Soul Ecology Service Practicum, Youth Leaders Action Camp, Soul Ecology Wisconsin, and the High School Projects Week.

ArtPlace

Location: Nationwide

Website: artplaceamerica.org

ArtPlace America (ArtPlace) is a ten year collaboration among a number of foundations, federal agencies, and financial institutions that works to position arts and culture as a core sector of comprehensive community planning and development in order to help strengthen the social, physical, and economic fabric of communities.

ArtPlace focuses its work on creative placemaking, which describes projects in which art plays an intentional and integrated role in place-based community planning and development. This brings artists, arts organizations, and artistic activity into the suite of placemaking strategies pioneered by Jane Jacobs and her colleagues, who believed that community development must be locally informed, human-centric, and holistic.

ArtPlace has national grants program that annually supports creative placemaking projects in communities of all sizes across the country.

ArtsMemphis

Location: Memphis, TN

Website: artsmemphis.org

We support the Memphis art, music and theatre community through engagement and participation. ArtsMemphis raises funds to ensure excellence in the arts and to build a vibrant cultural community for everyone. ArtsMemphis provides annual support, financial oversight, advocacy and mentoring to many diverse organizations through annual grants in several grant categories.

We fund arts education and outreach projects and oversee an Audience Development Initiative to enhance and build local cultural audiences. ArtsMemphis has allocated $40 million over the past 10 years to support our arts community. More than 95% of every dollar raised through the annual campaign is reinvested in the community through arts support.

Our mission is to use our funds to ensure excellence in the arts and build a vibrant cultural community for everyone. We were founded by volunteer community leaders in 1963.

Association for Community Design

Location: Nationwide

Website: communitydesign.org

Established in 1977, the Association for Community Design (ACD) is a network of individuals, organizations, and institutions committed to increasing the capacity of planning and design professions to better serve communities.

ACD serves and supports practitioners, educators, and organizations engaged in community-based design and planning.

ACD is incorporated as a 501(c)3 membership organization and is governed by a volunteer board of directors. Membership is open to both organizations and individuals.

The dues collected by the ACD support an annual conference, program development, and the maintenance of the website.

Association for Neighborhood and Housing Development

Location: New York, NY

Website: anhd.org

The Association for Neighborhood and Housing Development (ANHD) works to build the strength of the community development movement in New York City. ANHD was founded in 1974 with the mission to help low-income communities thrive and to ensure that all New Yorkers can live in decent, affordable housing and neighborhoods.

Today ANHD leads a membership of 99 of the City's leading community development and neighborhood-based not-for-profit affordable housing organizations. Our member groups use grassroots advocacy strength, bricks-and-mortar development skills, and focused neighborhood-level services to work for more decent, just and equitable communities.

ANHD supports our member groups with a mix of training, capacity-building resources, strategic research, and high-impact public policy advocacy campaigns. ANHD members groups have built over 100,000 affordable units in NYC in the past 25 years.

Avaaz

Location: International

Website: avaaz.org/en

Avaaz is a global web movement to bring people-powered politics to decision making everywhere. A transnational community that is more democratic, and could be more effective, than the United Nations. Avaaz—meaning "voice" in several European, Middle Eastern and Asian languages—launched in 2007 with a simple democratic mission: organize citizens of all nations to close the gap between the world we have and the world most people everywhere want.

Avaaz empowers millions of people from all walks of life to take action on pressing global, regional and national issues, from corruption and poverty to conflict and climate change. Our model of internet organising allows thousands of individual efforts, however small, to be rapidly combined into a powerful collective force.

Avaaz has a single, global team with a mandate to work on any issue of public concern-allowing campaigns of extraordinary nimbleness, flexibility, focus, and scale. We focus on tipping-point moments of crisis and opportunity.

Baltimore Slumlord Watch

Location: Baltimore, MD

Website: slumlordwatch.com

Baltimore Slumlord Watch was created in January of 2009, as a way for city residents to discuss and share information on Baltimore's many slumlords.

Started by a resident who was tired of watching out of town "investors" and others destroy neighborhoods as a result of their negligence, we hope this blog will serve as a valuable service to other city residents who are sick of the problems slumlords cause in our communities.

Please note, we do not work for realtors, developers, or property investors, and have no financial interest in property in Baltimore City.

Bay Area Council

Location: S.F. Bay area, CA

Website: bayareacouncil.org

The Bay Area Council is a business-sponsored, public policy advocacy organization for the nine-county Bay Area. The Council proactively advocates for a strong economy, a vital business environment, and a better quality of life for everyone who lives here. We are business leaders committed to working with public and civic leaders to make the Bay Area the most innovative, globally competitive, and sustainable region in the world.

Founded in 1945, as a way for the region's business community and like-minded individuals to concentrate and coordinate their efforts, the Bay Area Council is widely respected by elected officials, policy makers and other civic leaders as the regional voice of business in the Bay Area.

The Bay Area Council has continues to push for policies that have helped to build the Bay Area into the powerful region that it is today. From advocating for the extension of BART to San Jose to supporting urban infill development to pushing for legislation to help shield companies from cyber security threats, the Bay Area Council works across a wide range of policies.

Bay Lights

Location: San Francisco Bay, CA

Website: thebaylights.org

The Bay Lights is a site-specific monumental light sculpture and art installation on the San Francisco Bay Bridge.

The installation consists of lights placed along 1.8 miles (2.9 km) of the cables on the north side of the suspension span of the bridge between Yerba Buena Island and San Francisco. The installation will be controlled via a computer and will display changing patterns that are not meant to repeat.

The Bay Lights is the world's largest LED light sculpture, 1.8 miles wide and 500 feet high. Inspired by the Bay Bridge's 75th Anniversary, it's 25,000 white LED lights are individually programmed by artist Leo Villareal to create a never-repeating, dazzling display across the Bay Bridge West Span through 2015.

The Bay Lights is a monumental tour de force eight times the scale of the Eiffel Tower's 100th Anniversary lighting. Shining from dusk until 2:00 a.m. for two years, it will impact over 50 million people in the Bay Area, with billions more seeing it in the media and online. By conservative estimates, $97 million dollars will be added to the local economy.

BayShare

Location: S.F. Bay Area

Website: bayshare.org

BayShare is an advocacy organization whose mission is to make the Bay Area the best place on the planet for sharing. As this movement grows, BayShare will explore how city stakeholders and the sharing community can work together to help the "sharing economy" flourish in the Bay Area to benefit the city, businesses, and communities.

The organization looks to be a resource for the Mayor's Working Group on the Sharing Economy and it will also serve as a resource for the public by hosting events and providing educational materials so that more residents and businesses engage with this new economy. The sharing economy is a popular way for individuals, governments and businesses to access goods and services in new and less expensive ways.

Today people are bartering, lending, trading, gifting and swapping their homes, cars, power drills, skills and even extra time. Spurred by need and a shift in cultural values, and empowered by peer technologies and business models, the sharing economy is democratizing access to resources of all kinds.

Big Parade Los Angeles

Location: Los Angeles, CA

Website: bigparadela.tumblr.com

The Big Parade is a two-day walk in Los Angeles. It includes about 100 public stairways over 35 miles, from downtown to Mt. Hollywood.

The walk runs on a timetable, and is designed as a series of attached loops, so that people can come and go as they please - join us for a mile, an hour, or an epic. Along the way, there's music, art, history, guest speakers, and lots of surprises.

The Big Parade is 100% free (except for the pizza), no donations (again, except for the pizza), no sponsors, no merchandise - just a walk with friends and neighbors.

Despite the length (and uphill nature) of the journey, the Big Parade is meant to live up to its name — an event whose primary purpose is to entertain. The route is filled with talks and performances from local figures, and historical insights into the city's configuration.

BIMBY

Location: Great Britain

Website: bimby.org.uk

The "Beauty-In-My Backyard" (BIMBY) Housing Toolkit is a simple and practical online tool which enables communities, organisations, Local Authorities and developers to collectively or individually create a regional BIMBY Housing Manual. It is specifically designed to give both certainty to house builders, who can be sure of their housing's popularity, whilst also granting security to the community and local authority that new building projects will tie in with local preferences and needs.

Using the BIMBY Toolkit, you will be able to directly influence the quality and beauty of new housing by developing a BIMBY Housing Manual for your area. You will feel empowered to engage in the siting and design of new homes, by influencing the planning process in a positive, rather than negative way.

You will feel empowered to demand that any new homes planned in your area are well located and well designed, by influencing the planning process in a positive, rather than negative, way.

BlackNLA

Location: Los Angeles, CA

Website: blacknla.org

"When I started Black In Los Angeles (BlackNLA) in March of 2000, I did so to fulfill a personal need...the ability to find at "the drop of a hat" a African American physician, lawyer, black organization, or event that would be of interest to me and my friends. I found a lot of sites out there, but they were always hit and miss."

"Some would have businesses, some would have events but I didn't want to have to remember 20 different web addresses, I wanted the information and I wanted to be able to get to it in a relatively easy manner. The Los Angeles area has a large black population, but we tend to be scattered and divided by city and county lines, so with the start of a new millennium and its advancing technology now is the time to bring this community together."

"Welcome to BlackNLA.com – a website where blacks living, working and visiting the Los Angeles metropolitan area can get information that pertains to their interests and lifestyles. A place to share information, resources, advertise and to network."

BLDG Memphis

Location: Memphis, TN

Website: bldgmemphis.org

BLDG Memphis (Build. Live. Develop. Grow.) is a coalition for organizations and individuals who support the development and redevelopment of healthy, vibrant, attractive, and economically sustainable neighborhoods throughout the Memphis region. We accomplish this through policy and advocacy, community engagement and civic engagement and capacity building programs for community development organizations.

BLDG Memphis is the new organizational identity of Community Development Council of Greater Memphis, including the Livable Memphis program. Under this new banner, BLDG Memphis unifies and promotes the same priorities, including strengthening the community development industry in Memphis and focusing on growth and development issues – including land use and transportation – and on increasing public participation in planning and development decisions.

BLDG Memphis supports the revitalization of Memphis neighborhoods through public policy development and advocacy, organizational capacity building, and community education.

Blexit

Location: Minneapolis, MN

Website: blexitmn.org

Blexit is a grassroots nonprofit organization made of community members who are ready to address the inequity in our state and country. We gather to strategize ways to make an impact on the private and public sectors of our economy by investing in the Black community and divesting from systems that have benefited from our pain.

We are made up of participants who come to our meetings, volunteers who offer support, resources and labor, members who contribute financially each month and spread the word about our work, and leaders who help guide and steer our community towards its goals.

Let's start with the basics of what "hotboxing" is and why that matters. Think of how people like you and me choose where we want to live. Usually, we want to live near family, school, or work. And we probably want to live somewhere we can afford that is safe, has some good schools, and has a culture that makes us feel at home. All these wants seem reasonable, don't they? Hotboxing is about people and power. It's specifically about the power people have to choose where they want to live.

Blights out

Location: New Orleans, LA

Website: blightsout.org

Blights Out is a collaborative and creative initiative to unite residents, artists, architects, and organizers in the design of a new, inclusive model for development. Our experiential method of "performing architecture" guides us through the purchase, design, and restoration of a blighted structure into a cultural resource center that will seed creative action around issues of blight, disinvestment, and housing.

Blights Out will partner with a local community land trust as the cultural organizing arm of the permanently affordable housing movement to share the tools and inspiration for New Orleans residents to build the destinies of their own neighborhoods.

Blights Out produces public art inspired by neighborhood stories, architecture, and history, culled from the multi-disciplinary research and critical interactive strategies that we employ.Blights Out is a collaborative process, involving residents, artists, architects, and organizers, at all stages of conception and implementation.

BMe

Location: Philadelphia, Baltimore and Detroit

Website: bmecommunity.org

The BMe Leadership Awards (BMe stands for "black male engagement") are given to men who are working to make their communities stronger. Trabian Shorters, founder of BMe, said that "there are thousands of black men who are assets to their communities - and if the rest of us got behind people like these, the city would have more to celebrate."

BMe is a network of black men in Philadelphia, Detroit, and Baltimore, that includes professionals, academics, and organizers working on an assortment of community projects. "There is no cavalry coming to save the day in communities across America. The visionary leaders that many are waiting for are already here," said Shawn Dove of Open Society Foundations, which also funds BMe.

Chris Rabb, an adjunct faculty member at Temple University, was awarded $20,000 to develop workshops to teach social entrepreneurship to low-wealth individuals. Rabb, author of *Invisible Capital: How Unseen Forces Shape Entrepreneurial Opportunity*, said he shows people how to "build commonwealth enterprises" that produce benefits for the community.

Botanica

Location: Louisville, KY

Website: waterfrontgardens.org

The mission of Botanica is to develop experiences that promote appreciation and understanding of plants for a more harmonious and sustainable world. Our vision is to create a botanical garden and conservatory of extraordinary beauty that engages, enlightens and inspires people about plants and nature.

The seeds of Botanica grew out of three Louisville plant societies that gathered together to host a community educational event. In 1993, members of the three groups – The Louisville Area Iris Society, The Louisville Area Daylily Society, and Hostas of Kentuckiana – formed a new organization and selected the name, "Botanica". Its mission was to become an umbrella organization for the local gardening community by offering quality programs to educate the general public about home gardening.

Over the next several years Botanica brought a variety of speakers to Louisville to help enlighten, entertain and educate the community about the botanical world. In addition to hosting a popular lecture series, for six years Botanica was the presenter of the plant-lover's noteworthy Fleur de Lis Festival – a celebration of all things botanical.

Brain Drain

Location: St. Louis, MO

Website: braindrain.com

Brain Drain is the brainchild of a group of young people united by a love for St. Louis. Some of us met in college, while others of us became friends after graduating. We are the ones who stayed, and we are committed to reversing the trend of young people leaving St. Louis.

Brain Drain aims to influence the trajectory of this city we all now proudly call home — and show other young minds that they can, too. Our passions are urban ones and human ones. We are designers, architects, urban planners, journalists, educators, musicians, brewers, printers, archivists, builders, activists, organizers, mobilizers.

Our respective fields range from as technical as architecture and mechanical engineering to as creative as illustration and printmaking. We want to offer our diverse skills, backgrounds, and passions to solve real problems on a human scale. Brain Drain is the antidote to urban exodus. Representing young natives and transplants that call St. Louis City home, our projects revere the city's unique heritage while catalyzing its future.

Brooklyn Arts Council

Location: Brooklyn, NY

Website: brooklynartscoucil.org

Brooklyn Arts Council (BAC) is the arts council for the borough of Brooklyn. We bring leadership and energy to every part of Brooklyn's arts scene, supporting and connecting it all. It doesn't matter where you fit into the arts—artist, audience member, participant, venue, educator or supporter—we want you to create and experience the arts in every neighborhood of Brooklyn.

What drives BAC? Our impassioned belief in the intrinsic value of the arts and artists, as well as what they can do. Art has a unique ability to bridge cultures, inspiring positive transformation in individual lives and entire communities.

BAC gives grants, presents free and affordable arts events, trains artists and arts professionals, teaches students, incubates new projects and promotes artists and cultural groups across our borough. As Brooklyn's cultural anchor since 1966, BAC has also been the catalyst helping the arts community grow.

Build a Better Block

Location: Nationwide

Website: betterblock.org

The Better Block project started in 2010, when a group of
community organizers, neighbors, and property owners gathered
together to revitalize a single commercial block in an underused
neighborhood corridor.

The area was filled with vacant properties, wide streets, and few
amenities for people who lived within walking distance. The
group brought together all of the resources from the community
and converted the block into a walkable, bikeable neighborhood
destination for people of all ages complete with bike lanes, cafe
seating, trees, plants, pop-up businesses, and lighting.

The project was developed to show the city how the block could
be revived and improve area safety, health, and economics if
ordinances that restricted small business and multi-modal
infrastructure were removed. Since that time, Better Block
projects have been developed throughout the world with many
of the temporary infrastructure improvements and businesses
made permanent.

Build a Better Burb

Location: Nationwide

Website: buildabetterburb.org

Build a Better Burb is an online publication dedicated to improving suburban design and planning. It uses engaging visuals to help suburban residents and leaders explore solutions from across the country that can be applied to their communities. By showcasing innovative ideas and outstanding projects, the site seeks to inspire conversation about the importance of design and planning within suburban communities.

The articles on the site highlight bold ideas for improving housing, regional planning, parking and transit, and a sense of place within suburban downtowns and neighborhoods. The Build a Better Burb website evolved from a design competition that was sponsored by the Long Island Index in 2010. The Build a Better Burb competition called for bold ideas from architects, urban designers, planners, and visionaries for the underutilized land in Long Island's downtowns.

The goal was to reimagine what might be possible for our region while seeing the scope of the problems facing Long Island.

Built Environment Forum Scotland

Location: Scotland

Website: befs.org.uk

The Built Environment Forum Scotland (BEFS) is the strategic intermediary body for Scotland's built environment sector, bringing together voluntary and professional non-governmental organisations that operate at the national level.

As an umbrella organisation, BEFS informs, mediates and advocates on strategic issues and policies affecting the built environment, historic and contemporary. Adopting a holistic approach, our aim is to put people at the heart of places that are both valued and of the highest possible quality.

BEFS strives to be recognised as the organisation that offers collective informed independent opinion on issues affecting the historic and contemporary built environment, to communicate information, opinion and good practice about the historic and built environment effectively with members, their constituents and across the sector, to support member organisations to build their capacity and operate more strategically and efficiently, and to develop a viable organisation by ensuring there is a responsive structure with appropriate skills and resources to deliver the outputs required to realise the vision.

Built: LA

Location: Los Angeles,CA

Website: cityhubla.github.io/LA_Building_Age/

Construction in Los Angeles may have exploded during the postwar era, but as a new interactive map shows, the wide age range of its buildings might surprise you. Using open data from local governments, built: LA visualizes the age of roughly 3 million buildings across L.A. County constructed between 1890 and 2008.

Drag your mouse to explore the vast web of communities and neighborhoods, hover over individual properties to discover what year they were created, and double click to zoom in further. Perhaps best of all, hit the rainbow stopwatch to view a decade-by-decade timelapse of development across the county. The city's core, in particular, clusters together buildings of century-spanning generations, while suburbs and communities to the east and west tend to represent just one or two decades of development.

Business Alliance for Local Living Economies

Location: Nationwide

Website: bealocalist.org

The Business Alliance for Local Living Economies (BALLE), represents thousands of communities and conveners, entrepreneurs, investors and funders who are defying business as usual. Our mission is to create local economies that work for all.

As we scan the horizon, we see gaps across systems. Dots to connect. We spark and deepen relationships among a growing movement of people using business to create healthy, equitable communities. Fierce love and confidence in our local economy framework drives us. Creating an economy that works for all is challenging, complex, and required.

We highlight those stories and the people, places, businesses, and organizations that are bringing the new economy to life. BALLE is shifting dollars from destructive and extractive "business as usual" to models that are healthy, equitable, and generative. We believe in building businesses that protect what we love, and that inspire each of us to be our best selves.

C40

Location: International

Website: c40.org

The C40 Cities Climate Leadership Group, connects more than 80 of the world's greatest cities, representing 600+ million people and one quarter of the global economy. Created and led by cities, C40 is focused on tackling climate change and driving urban action that reduces greenhouse gas emissions and climate risks, while increasing the health, wellbeing and economic opportunities of urban citizens.

C40 was founded on the idea that cities can achieve more by working together than acting alone. C40's international staff supports mayors of the world's megacities to deliver bold, ambitious and transformational action on climate change, through the exchange of ideas, programmes and policies; world class research; technical expertise; events that convene the world's foremost climate experts and communications support to highlight the individual achievements and collective leadership of cities.

Member cities have already committed to reducing their emissions by a total of more than 3 gigatons of CO_2 by 2030 – the equivalent of taking 600 million cars off the road.

California Alliance for Boys and Men of Color

Location: California

Website: allianceforbmoc.org

All Californians stand to benefit by doing everything possible to ensure that young men of color have the chance to grow up healthy, to get a good education, and to make positive contributions to their communities. We will reap the rewards of this investment.

The Alliance is working to ensure that California's boys and young men of color live in safe neighborhoods, succeed in school and work, and possess the knowledge, skills, and leadership capacity to contribute to their families, communities, and the state's social and economic well-being.

Working at the local and state level, the Alliance is actively pursuing reforms that will; increase access to health services that recognize the strengths and assets of boys and young men of color while also responding to the trauma and chronic adversity that many face, achieve 100 percent high-school graduation rates among boys and young men of color by strengthening the performance of public schools and reducing expulsion rates and ensure boys and young men of color live in safe neighborhoods and can attend safe schools.

California ReLeaf

Location: California

Website: californiareleaf.org

California ReLeaf works statewide to promote alliances among community-based groups, individuals, industry, and government agencies, encouraging each to contribute to the livability of our cities and the protection of our environment by planting and caring for trees.

California ReLeaf also serves as the State's volunteer coordinator for urban forestry in partnership with the California Department of Forestry and Fire Protection.

Our mission is the expanding delivery of services and resources to California ReLeaf network groups, broadening funding opportunities for urban and community forestry projects, fostering involvement within the urban forestry movement throughout California's diverse communities and improving legislative outreach and efforts on a state and federal level.

Campaign to Protect Rural England

Location: England, UK

Website: cpre.org.uk

The Campaign to Protect Rural England (CPRE) believes a beautiful, thriving countryside is important for everyone, no matter where they live. Millions of town and city dwellers recharge their batteries with a walk or a bike ride in the local Green Belt, spend weekends and holidays in our National Parks, or enjoy fresh local produce. People who live in rural areas keep our countryside beautiful and productive.

The countryside is unique, essential, precious and finite – and it's in danger. Every year, a little more is lost forever to urban sprawl, new roads, housing and other developments. Rural shops and services are closing, and increasingly intensive farming is changing the character of the countryside. Climate change, too, will have serious impacts on the rural environment. CPRE works locally and nationally to stand up for the countryside: to protect it from the threats it faces, and to shape its future for the better.

CPRE has been standing up for the countryside for over 80 years. In that time, we've seen some remarkable successes. We've helped win protection as national parks for some of our most remarkable landscapes.

Cape Action for People and the Environment

Location: Cape Town, South Africa

Website: https://www.thegef.org/project/cape-biodiversity-conservation-and-sustainable-development-project

Cape Action for People and the Environment (CAPE) is a 20 year partnership of government and civil society aimed at conserving and restoring the biodiversity of the Cape Floristic Region and the adjacent marine environment, while delivering significant benefits to the people of the region.

The rationale of the CAPE partnership is to create linkages between government, the private sector and civil society so that we all work together with a common strategy, avoiding duplication, addressing gaps and uniting to leverage resources and to tackle agreed common priorities in terms of a shared vision.

The CAPE programme is coordinated through the CAPE Coordination Unit which is hosted by the South African National Biodiversity Institute (SANBI) and its Fynbos Programme.

Capitol Riverfront

Location: Washington, DC

Website: capitolriverfront.org

The river and its renewal are at the heart of the Capitol Riverfront, offering impressive vistas and unique opportunities for recreation and waterfront living. Rising from the foundations of its 19th-century heritage as a shipbuilding and maritime powerhouse, the riverfront today is leading the way in riverfront renewal and green innovation. Here green is more than a color—it is a commitment evident in sustainable development, environmentally conscious businesses, mass transit access, walkability, and active public parks.

The Capitol Riverfront has 30+ LEED certified existing or planned buildings, the largest green roof in DC (on the U.S. DOT building), the first LEED certified ballpark, a LEED Neighborhood Development project at The Yards, the largest LEED for homes project in the country at Capitol Quarter, four new parks including Canal Park designed to be a model of sustainability, and streetscape built with larger tree boxes and permeable pavers to collect stormwater runoff and increase the green canopy.

Cleaning the river is a task that will take years to complete but is already underway and progress continues to be made.

Catalytic Communities

Location: Rio de Janeiro, Brazil

Website: catcomm.org

Based in Rio de Janeiro, Catalytic Communities (CatComm) is an empowerment, communications, think tank and advocacy NGO run as a small, adaptive collaborative network which works to support and empower residents of informal settlements. As needs among favela residents and their leaders evolve, we do too.

CatComm functions as a news source, agenda-setter, movement-builder and research collaborative, each to a lesser or greater extent at any time, as needs dictate. We are the only organization in Rio working at the intersection of community development, international networks, media and urban planning.

For 13 years we have been supporting community organizing efforts across Rio de Janeiro by developing and providing access to communications and networking tools and spaces supporting favela development tailored in strategic ways when the time is right.

CatComm is classified as a 501(c)3 not-for-profit organization in the United States, in addition to our charity status in Brazil.

Causa Justa :: Just Cause

Location: San Francisco Bay Area, CA

Website: cjjc.org

Causa Justa :: Just Cause builds grassroots power and leadership to create strong, equitable communities.

Born from a visionary merger between a Black organization and a Latino immigrant organization, we build bridges of solidarity between working class communities of color. Through rights-based services, policy campaigns, civic engagement, and direct action, we improve conditions in our neighborhoods in the San Francisco Bay Area, and contribute to building the larger multi-racial, multi-generational movement needed for fundamental change.

We envision equal rights for people of color, immigrants, women, and all oppressed and exploited people. We envision an end to racism, and want to build a society based on self-determination, social justice, and solidarity. We envision a future without displacement through real estate speculation and forced migration. We envision a society where housing is a human right and all families thrive.

Center for Community Progress

Location: Nationwide

Website: communityprogress.net

Founded in 2010, the Center for Community Progress (CCP) is the only national 501(c)3 nonprofit organization solely dedicated to building a future in which entrenched, systemic blight no longer exists in American communities. The mission of CCP is to ensure that communities have the vision, knowledge, and systems to transform blighted, vacant, and other problem properties into assets supporting neighborhood vitality.

As a national leader on solutions for blight and vacancy, CCP serves as the leading resource for local, state and federal policies and best practices that address the full cycle of property revitalization, from blight prevention, through the acquisition and maintenance of problem properties, to their productive reuse.

CCP provides technical assistance to communities nationwide, hosts the national Reclaiming Vacant Properties Conference, and offers numerous other resources and services to help communities transform blighted properties into community assets.

Center for Great Neighborhoods

Location: Covington, KY

Website: greatneighborhoods.org

The Center began in 1976 when the Fourth Street Center and Downtown Neighborhood Center merged to become the Covington Community Center. In the late 1960s and early 1970s these two small neighborhood centers were created by separate churches in Covington. Both served the emergency needs of low income residents, provided recreation activities for youth and helped residents address community issues. The merger helped create a single, strong organization with a mission to serve those same needs.

Community starts with US and everything we do is centered around this idea. The Center is a catalyst for positive growth in Covington but our role is only one part of the equation. Our most important partner is YOU and the other residents of Covington.

How do we do it? We spark this growth by bringing people together, encouraging them to work with each other, and supporting their efforts to shape the future of their community. Why do we do it? We are committed to helping people discover and develop their skills, find and use the resources they need.

Center for Neighborhood Technology

Location: Nationwide

Website: cnt.org

Founded in 1978, the Center for Neighborhood Technology (CNT) has been a leader in promoting more livable and sustainable urban communities. In fact, our work focused on sustainable development before the term became as popular as it is today. As a creative think-and-do-tank, we research, invent, and test urban strategies that use resources more efficiently and more equitably.

Over the years, CNT's work, especially in the areas of climate, energy, water, transportation and community development, has paid off by fueling a generation of community development and learning institutions, earning CNT a reputation as an economic innovator and leader in the field of creative sustainable development. CNT is an "innovations center for urban sustainability."

We approach our work by participating in three primary activities: researching urban problems to build knowledge through tools and activities that change how residents, policymakers, and market actors respond to issues such as efficient use of resources, strategies for reducing pollution, or ways to improve public transportation.

Center for Opportunity Urbanism

Location: International

Website: opportunityurbanism.org

The Center for Opportunity Urbanism (COU) closely examines how planning and zoning decisions can hamper or spark economic growth. It will also highlight key demographic concerns, notably around the critical issue of families, who generally seek out housing that is both affordable and spacious enough to raise children, and governance – the question of who makes decisions about the commons – will also be a key area of exploration.

COU promulgates a perspective on urban development that is applicable to most American cities, and indeed to cities around the world. Initially COU will be seeking to define this new model with comparative studies of different regions in terms of how they most efficiently address issues ranging from promoting upward mobility and reducing poverty, including among minorities, and spark broad-based economic growth.

It will be the primary task of the COU to spell out how cities can drive opportunity for the bulk of their citizens. Initially, at least, this will be primarily a virtual, media-centered effort.

Center for Sustainable Engagement and Development

Location: New Orleans, LA

Website: sustainthenine.org

Founded in December 2006, the Lower 9th Ward Center for Sustainable Engagement and Development (CSED) is a 501(c)3 grassroots organization devoted to restoring New Orleans' Lower Ninth Ward as a safe, environmentally just and economically vibrant community – and one of the first to become carbon-neutral in North America.

Born in the aftermath of catastrophic flooding in the Lower Ninth Ward caused by the failure of the federal levee system following Hurricanes Katrina and Rita, CSED provides community-based support to residents of the Lower Ninth Ward – from "River to Bayou" – in all aspects of sustainability for area neighborhoods as part of long-term recovery and rebuilding efforts.

Our mission is to stimulate civic engagement, repopulate, sustain natural systems, assist community leadership and preserve resources in the Lower 9th Ward neighborhoods. Our goal is the re-creation and repopulation of a strong community, mindful of its resources and vulnerabilities, with an engaged citizenry.

Center for Transit Oriented Development

Location: Nationwide

Website: ctod.org

The Center for Transit Oriented Development (CTOD) is the leading national entity dedicated to providing innovative practices, policy reform, research, analysis, and investment tools to support TOD implementation. CTOD is particularly attuned to opportunities to leverage and catalyze market interests to support TOD, while also identifying the mechanisms through which benefits can be shared equitably by low and moderate-income people.

CTOD partners with the public, private, and philanthropic sectors to foster high-performing communities around transit stations and to build transit systems that maximize community and economic development potential utilizing the full opportunity created by the existing or proposed transit network.

CTOD works to integrate local and regional planning to generate new tools for economic development, real estate and investment issues, improve affordability and livability for all members of the community, and respond to imperatives for climate change and sustainability.

Center for Urban Design and Mental Health

Location: International

Website: urbandesignmentalhealth.com

The Centre for Urban Design and Mental Health (UD/MH) is a start-up think tank focused on answering one question: how can we design better mental health into our cities?

More people are living and working in urban environments than ever before - and these environments affect how we feel. Urban design by architects, transport designers, city planners, developers, interior designers, urban gardeners, street artists, and many more impact our mental health as we move around our built environments.

UD/MH reviews the breadth of research on urban design and mental health, summarizes, and identifies gaps, catalyzes interdisciplinary dialogue on urban design and mental health in cities around the world, showcases successful projects and innovative ideas and develops practical, evidence-based recommendations to improve mental health and reduce mental illness through urban design. UD/MH brings together useful research, ideas, experiences and intelligence from across the world and shares it on our platforms.

Center for Urban Pedagogy

Location: New York, NY

Website: welcometocup.org

The Center for Urban Pedagogy (CUP) is a nonprofit organization that uses design and art to improve civic engagement. CUP projects demystify the urban policy and planning issues that impact our communities, so that more individuals can better participate in shaping them. We believe that increasing understanding of how these systems work is the first step to better and more diverse community participation.

CUP projects are collaborations of art and design professionals, community-based advocates and policymakers, and our staff. Together we take on complex issues—from the juvenile justice system to zoning law to food access—and break them down into simple, accessible, visual explanations.

The tools we create are used by organizers and educators all over New York City and beyond to help their constituents better advocate for their own community needs. Community Education works with advocacy organizations, policy experts, and designers to produce publications, workshops, and other teaching tools that explain important policy issues for the people who most need to know.

Center for Urban Science and Progress

Location: New York, NY

Website: cusp.nyu.edu

The Center for Urban Science and Progress (CUSP) is a unique
public-private research center that uses New York City as its
laboratory and classroom to help cities around the world become
more productive, livable, equitable, and resilient. CUSP observes,
analyzes, and models cities to optimize outcomes, prototype new
solutions, formalize new tools and processes, and develop new
expertise/experts. These activities will make CUSP the world's
leading authority in the emerging field of "Urban Informatics."

CUSP aims to unite two extraordinarily profound developments
in human history in order to improve the lives of citizens around
the globe. 90 percent of the world's data has been created in the
last two years alone. For the first time in history, more than half
the world's population lives in urban areas.

CUSP will instrument New York City and use existing data from a
network of agencies to transform the city into a living laboratory
and classroom. It will make sense of the vast amount of data it
collects to help cities around the world become more productive,
more livable, more equitable, and more resilient.

CEOs for Cities

Location: Nationwide

Website: ceosforcities.org

Today, a city's future relies upon engaged organizational leaders from across sectors with a shared agenda and a coherent voice. With more than 250 partners from over 40 cities, CEOs for Cities is a civic innovation lab and network of urban leaders and change agents from diverse sectors, including business, higher education, economic development, cultural and creative sectors, foundations and government- dedicated to building, advancing, and sustaining the next generation of great American cities.

Our customers are urban leaders, and we honor leadership where it happens, regardless of rank or sector. Our theory of change is that at a time when more than half of the world lives in urban areas, strong, successful American cities are more essential than ever to a strong America. And at a time when our federal and state governments too often are dysfunctional, cities are the best scale at which to organize to tackle critical issues.

Our value proposition is that we are a platform that serves as a connected, cross-sector, cross-generational, collaborative infrastructure for making cities better and more successful places to live and work - places where you can build your business and love your life.

Challenge Detroit

Location: Detroit, MI

Website: challengedetroit.org

Challenge Detroit is a leadership and professional development program that has invited 30 of tomorrow's leaders to live, work, play, and give in and around the greater Detroit area for one year. Can retaining and attracting 30 of the best and brightest innovative thinkers really make a difference? Detroit is betting on it. Challenge Detroit fellows have the courage, passion, and drive to make a difference. Combine this with a community-wide effort of highly connected, motivated, creative, innovative thinkers, and the formula will be explosive!

Fellows will receive incentives to live in selected areas of Detroit. All 30 fellows will work approximately 32 hours per week at their host company for an entire year.

To strengthen the bond between the 30 fellows while demonstrating the positive qualities of the region, Challenge Detroit, along with local organizations, will make monthly social and cultural activities happen. The 30 will participate in monthly team challenges designed to positively impact the community while keeping the fellows as well as the followers of Challenge Detroit engaged.

Chesapeake Bay Foundation

Location: Chesapeake Bay– DE, MD, VA

Website: cbf.org

In the four centuries since the explorations of Captain John Smith, the Chesapeake Bay has lost half of its forested shoreline, more than half its wetlands, nearly 80 percent of its underwater grasses, and more than 98 percent of its oysters. Across the watershed, approximately 1.7 million acres of once-untouched land were developed by 1950.

Development has accelerated dramatically since then, with an additional 2.7 million acres built on or paved over between 1950 and 1980. The human pressure of these changes has imposed heavy negative impacts on the health and resilience of the Bay. Although we will never return to the pristine territory explored by Captain John Smith during those early voyages, Chesapeake Bay Foundation (CBF) is fighting to return this fragile ecosystem to balance.

For years, CBF has been a leader in restoration efforts that improve the capacity of rivers, streams, and the Bay to treat pollution. In programs across the watershed, many of them conducted with CBF volunteers and partner organizations, CBF is restoring native oysters, planting underwater grasses, and planting trees, to restore the Bay's natural filters.

Chicago Architecture Foundation

Location: Chicago, IL

Website: architecture.org

The Chicago Architecture Foundation (CAF) is a nonprofit organization that inspires people to discover why design matters. CAF offers tours, exhibitions, adult and youth education programs and a retail shop. Admission to our exhibitions is free. Most of our adult programs and family programs are free and open to the public. Tour prices vary. Unless otherwise stated in the program or exhibition details, all programs and exhibitions are held at CAF, 224 South Michigan Avenue. See a map of our facilities for specific locations within the building.

Most of our adult programs and family programs are free and open to the public. Please refer to the adult programs or family programs section of our main website for detailed information.

Discounted parking is available for CAF members at the Millennium Park parking garage or Grant Park South parking garage.

Chicago Central Area Committee

Location: Chicago, IL

Website: ccac.org

Chicago Central Area Committee (CCAC) is a 50 year old civic group comprised of the City's business and cultural leaders devoted to making Chicago a better place to live, work, visit and conduct business. The CCAC is committed to enhancing the City's global competitiveness and quality of life, translating that vision into physical plans, and taking the necessary collaborative actions to implement those plans.

CCAC played a key role in the development of the current "Chicago 2020 Plan"

Representing a mix of interests, the CCAC acknowledges the importance of developing a first-class infrastructure of environmental, transportation, telecommunications, energy, and open space systems. These elements will combine to form a high-quality, high-energy, 24-hour Central Area urban environment that reinforces Chicago's place as a global city in the 21st century.

CicLAvia

Location: Los Angeles, CA

Website: ciclavia.org

CicLAvia catalyzes vibrant public spaces, active transportation and good health through car-free streets.

CicLAvia engages with people to transform our relationship with our communities and with each other.

CicLAvia makes the streets safe for people to walk, skate, play and ride a bike. There are activities along the route. Shop owners and restaurants are encouraged to open their doors to people along the CicLAvia. Ciclovías started in Bogotá, Colombia, over thirty years ago as a response to the congestion and pollution of city streets. Now they happen throughout Latin America and the United States.

By connecting communities and giving people a break from the stress of car traffic, the health benefits are immense. Ciclovías bring families outside of their homes to enjoy the streets, our largest public space. In Los Angeles we need CicLAvia more than ever.

Citizens Institute for Rural Design

Location: Nationwide

Website: rural-design.org

Rural design is an important tool for rural communities to build upon existing assets and improve the way a community looks, its quality of life, and its economic viability. However, few rural communities have access to design assistance or the expertise to tackle these challenges on their own.

The Citizens' Institute on Rural Design (CIRD) provides communities access to the resources they need to convert their own good ideas into reality. CIRD works with communities with populations of 50,000 or less, and offers annual competitive funding to as many as four small towns or rural communities to host a two-and-a-half day community design workshop.

With support from a wide range of design, planning and creative placemaking professionals, the workshops bring together local leaders from non-profits, community organizations, and government to develop actionable solutions to the community's pressing design challenges. The community receives additional support through webinars, conference calls, and web-based resources.

Citizens Union

Location: New York, NY

Website: citizensunion.org

Citizens Union is a nonpartisan good government group dedicated to making democracy work for all New Yorkers. Citizens Union serves as a civic watchdog, combating corruption and fighting for political reform. We work to ensure fair and open elections, honest and efficient government, and a civically-engaged public. We are New Yorkers from diverse backgrounds and political beliefs, connected to our communities and united in our commitment to put the city's long-term interest ahead of all special interests.

Principled and pragmatic, Citizens Union is an independent force for constructive reform, driving policy and educating the public to achieve accountable government in the City and State of New York.

Citizens Union of the City of New York is a 501(c)4 organization that advances legislation to improve our government and political system, and conducts evaluations of candidates for city and state offices. Citizens Union Foundation is a 501(c)3 organization that conducts in-depth research on public policy, provides information to the public, and promotes public policy solutions.

CITY2.0

Location: International

Website: tedcity2.org

The City 2.0 website is a platform created to surface the myriad stories and collective actions being taken by citizens around the world.

We draw on the best of what is already being discovered by urban advocates and add grassroots movers and shakers into the mix. What's emerging is a complex picture of the future city--a place more playful, more safe, more beautiful, and more healthy for everyone.

Our website contains some tips for how you can enliven our site with your inspiration, stories, and projects. This site is most fundamentally about city dwellers, urban entrepreneurs, organizers, dreamers and doers.

This is the best space to tell us who you are. What is a city, after all, without its citizens? This is the best space for brief thoughts, favorite quotes, snapshots etc. Think of it as your own urban focused Twitter.

City Atlas

Location: New York, NY

Website: newyork.thecityatlas.org

City Atlas is a New Yorker's comprehensive guide to events, ideas and actions that are positively impacting and forming our city's future.

We like to think of ourselves as a bottom-up sustainability plan for New York City that works best with your participation. The Atlas reflects the good work that individuals, organizations, businesses, cultural institutions, and everyone else (!) does to move our city toward a more sustainable version of itself.

Basically, we aggregate a lot of good stuff and show you how some of our lived culture is already moving us in the right direction.

City Atlas is built by and for New Yorkers and just like this city, it relies on science, creativity, and community.

CityFix

Location: International

Website: thecityfix.com

The CityFix is an online resource for learning about the latest in sustainable urban mobility and planning. Launched in 2007, the site connects a global network of writers, urban planners, designers, engineers, and citizens who work to make cities better places to live.

EMBARQ is a not-for-profit program of the World Resources Institute that works to catalyze and help implement environmentally, socially, and financially sustainable transport and urban planning solutions.

Since 2002, the EMBARQ network has grown to include six centers – based in Brazil, China, India, Mexico, Turkey and the Andean region, that work together with local authorities, businesses and national governments to reduce pollution, improve public health, and create safe and accessible urban environments. TheCityFix relies on this international community and other volunteer contributors to provide a global, multi-disciplinary perspective to its coverage of issues relating to urban sustainability.

City of the Year

Location: International

Website: online.wsj.com/ad/cityoftheyear

In 2012, Citibank and the Marketing Services Department of Wall Street Journal Magazine teamed up with the Urban Land Institute (ULI) to determine which city— wherever in the world— deserved the title "Innovative City of the Year." For the first round, ULI produced a list of 200 contenders, we then asked readers of WSJ Magazine and others to vote on the city that deserved the title. The original list of 200 was reduced to 25. We then asked readers and others to vote again and the list was narrowed to three finalists.

Events were held in each of the finalist cities where we encouraged civic leaders and business executives to use social media to spread the word. Our Number One city was so proud of their accomplishments that response was overwhelming. Originally distinguished for its progress and potential, the winning city found new solutions to classic problems of mobility and environmental sustainability.

Today, gondolas and a giant escalator shuttle citizens from steep mountainside homes to jobs and schools in the valley below.

City Parks Alliance

Location: Nationwide

Website: cityparksalliance.org

The City Parks Alliance (CPA) is a national organization comprised of city parks leaders from across the country who work together to strengthen America's city parks. The organization has been in formation over the past several years in response to a broad-based movement of city park advocates who recognize the critical role parks play in the revitalization of our cities.

The mission of CPA is to create vibrant and healthy parks and green spaces that contribute to sustainable cities by organizing, facilitating and nurturing a broad-based movement.

A group of parks administrators and advocates began meeting in 1999 to establish greater collaboration and discuss the formation of a new national entity. A little over a year later while meeting in Philadelphia, this group endorsed the creation of the CPA in 2000.

The group's creation is an outgrowth of the Lila Wallace-Reader's Digest Funds' Urban Parks Initiative, which helped establish a network of top non-profit and public-sector urban parks organizations, and city parks and recreation agencies.

CityVision

Location: Washington, D.C.

Website: nbm.org/learn/schools-teachers

Now in its seventeenth year, CityVision is an award-winning outreach program that uses design as a framework to teach District of Columbia public school students how to become active participants in shaping their communities. Through extensive fieldwork and careful mentoring at the National Building Museum, students identify needs and propose solutions designed to help local neighborhoods.

In CityVision, participants: develop problem solving and critical thinking skills, learn technical skills, including sketching and architectural drawing, photography, scale, and model building, practice negotiation and collaboration while working as a team, sharpen public speaking and communication skills, and explore careers in architecture, engineering, construction and design.

CityVision takes place during the fall and spring of the academic year, and is made possible by a close collaboration between the National Building Museum and D.C. Public Schools and Public Charter Schools. Each year, junior high and middle schools integrate CityVision as part of their curriculum and offer participating students with academic credit.

CIVITAS

Location: Manhattan, NY

Website: civitasnyc.org

We are a union of citizens dedicated to improving neighborhood quality of life in the Upper East Side and East Harlem since 1981.

CIVITAS promotes urban planning, zoning and land use policies that are sensible and sensitive to residential life in our neighborhoods. CIVITAS supports environmentally sound development, vibrant retail activity at street level, uncluttered sidewalks and access to good public transit.

CIVITAS opposes overbearing towers that are non-contextual and cut off light and air from surrounding buildings and the sidewalk below. CIVITAS commissions urban planning studies, speaks out at public hearings, issues reports and keeps its members informed on current issues impacting on urban life, including traffic congestion, historic preservation, zoning variances, water quality and public access to parks and the waterfront.

The mission of CIVITAS is to foster, mobilize and coordinate civic concern.

Clean Water Action

Location: Nationwide

Website: cleanwateraction.org

Clean Water Action i(CWA) s a one million member organization of diverse people and groups joined together to protect our environment, health, economic well-being and community quality of life.

CWA's goals include clean, safe and affordable water, prevention of health threatening pollution, creation of environmentally safe jobs and businesses and empowerment of people to make democracy work.

CWA organizes strong grassroots groups and coalitions and campaigns to elect environmental candidates and solve environmental and community problems.

Coalition for Non-Profit Housing and Economic Development

Location: Washington, DC

Website: cnhed.org

The Coalition for Non-Profit Housing and Economic Development (CNHED) leads nonprofit community development organizations in ensuring that residents with low and moderate incomes have housing and economic opportunities in neighborhoods throughout the District.

CNHED is a dynamic, member-driven 501(c)3 umbrella organization that supports the nonprofit housing and economic development industry in Washington, DC.

Since its inception in 2000, the organization has grown from 55 organizations to over 130 today, due in part to its success in carrying out a highly successful program of advocacy, training, research, communication, and information sharing in support of its members. CNHED's membership represents a broad spectrum of entities including nonprofit and for-profit affordable housing developers, housing counseling and service agencies, community development corporations, small businesses, lenders, intermediaries, associations and government agencies.

Coalition of Community Development Financial Institutions

Location: Nationwide

Website: cdfi.org

The Coalition of Community Development Financial Institutions (CCDFI) is the unified national voice of community development financial institutions.

Our mission is to encourage fair access to financial resources for America's underserved people and communities Nationwide, over 1000 CDFIs serve economically distressed communities by providing credit, capital and financial services that are often unavailable from mainstream financial institutions. CDFIs have loaned and invested billions in our nation's most distressed communities. Even better, their loans and investments have leveraged billions more dollars from the private sector for development activities in low wealth communities across the nation.

The CCDFI advocates on behalf of the CDFI industry and educates the public about community development finance. We are a primary source of information and knowledge about the CDFI field for the general public, the media, public officials, and private sector lenders.

CommUniverCity San Jose

Location: San Jose, CA

Website: cucsj.org

CommUniverCity San José believes that everyone deserves to live in vibrant, healthy, and engaged communities.

Every day we work with residents to develop great neighborhoods, because no one's opportunities in life should be limited by the place where they live.

We do this by engaging residents and students in service learning projects that accomplish neighborhood-driven goals through a cross-sector partnership with the City of San José, the residents of Central San José neighborhoods, and San José State University students.

Communities for a Better Environment

Location: California

Website: cbecal.org

Founded in 1978, Communities for a Better Environment (CBE) is one of the preeminent environmental justice organizations in the nation. The mission of CBE is to build people's power in California's communities of color and low income communities to achieve environmental health and justice by preventing and reducing pollution and building green, healthy and sustainable communities and environments.

CBE provides residents in blighted and heavily polluted urban communities in California with organizing skills, leadership training and legal, scientific and technical assistance, so that they can successfully confront threats to their health and well-being.

CBE's vision embraces local transformation, but the CBE vision goes far beyond local as humanity now faces environmental crisis of global proportions. The earth's most vulnerable populations experience the greatest suffering from environmental degradation. Climate change has triggered deadly drought, water shortages and wildfires, air and water pollution, threatens food supplies and our entire way of life.

Community Heart and Soul

Location: Nationwide

Website:
https://www.orton.org/build-your-community/communit
y-heart-soul/

We identify what's possible and inspire hope and aspiration through actively seeking the collective wisdom of all residents, including those whose voices are often missing, Community Heart and Soul (CHS) brings people together to build stronger, healthier and more economically vibrant small cities and towns based on what matters most to everyone.

Developed and field-tested over a decade in partnership with small cities and towns, CHS has evolved into a proven model for engaging a community in shaping the future.

By following a four phase, step-by-step model, residents are able to bring the community together to chart a course forward that recognizes the unique character of the place and the emotional connection of the people who live there.

Community Solutions

Location: Nationwide

Website: cmtysolutions.org

Community Solutions (CS) is a national not-for-profit organization whose mission is to strengthen communities to end homelessness. Based in New York city, CS partners with community leaders, public agencies, non-profits, property developers and health and human services organizations to create practical, scalable, cost effective solutions to homelessness. .

As the national spinoff of Common Ground, a pioneer and leader in the field, our perspective is based on twenty years of experience ending street homelessness, developing and operating permanent supportive housing, and bringing a range of community stakeholders together to create and share cost-effective solutions to support our most vulnerable neighbors.

Our goal is to accelerate change by bringing proven, replicable innovations that end homelessness to a national scale, working with what we call "tipping point" communities, as well as to advance new models of homelessness prevention and community development.

Community Voices Heard

Location: New York City, NY

Website: cvhaction.org

Community Voices Heard (CVH) is a member-led multiracial organization, principally of women of color and low-income families in New York State, that builds power to secure social, economic and racial justice for all. We accomplish this through grassroots organizing, leadership development, policy changes, and creating new models of direct democracy.

CVH is working towards building a society in which the systems that govern us foster racial, social and economic justice not exploitation – particularly for low-income people of color. We seek a society in which all people – regardless of their race, ethnicity, religion, age, gender expression, sexual identity, citizen status, primary language, and ability – are treated with mutual respect and when privileges of one group do not exist.

CVH seeks a society in which all people are able to work with dignity, have access to a sustainable quality of life, and can obtain unconditional support in their time of need. We seek a society in which governmental structures are transparent and based on community needs.

Commute Seattle

Location: Seattle, WA

Website: commuteseatlle.org

Commute Seattle is a not-for-profit transportation management association (TMA) working to provide alternatives to drive-alone commute trips into Downtown Seattle's 10 neighborhoods. We are a 501c(4) not-for-profit, public-private partnership commissioned, funded, and governed by an advisory board of executive leaders from the Downtown Seattle Association, King County Metro, and the City of Seattle.

We seek to reduce the drive-alone commute rate in downtown Seattle, making Seattle a strong leader among peer cities in supporting alternatives to driving alone.

Commute Seattle is committed to delivering transportation services that not only reduce congestion and support increased commuter options, but also support business objectives in the greater downtown area.

Cooperation Jackson

Location: Jackson, MS

Website: cooperationjackson.org

Cooperation Jackson is an emerging vehicle for sustainable community development, economic democracy, and community ownership. Our vision is to develop a cooperative network based in Jackson, Mississippi that will consist of four interconnected and interdependent institutions: an emerging federation of local worker cooperatives, a developing cooperative incubator, a cooperative education and training center (the Lumumba Center for Economic Democracy and Development), and a cooperative bank or financial institution.

Cooperation Jackson's basic theory of change is centered on the position that organizing and empowering the structurally under and unemployed sectors of the working class, particularly from Black and Latino communities, to build worker organized and owned cooperatives will be a catalyst for the democratization of our economy and society overall.

Cooperation Jackson believes that we can replace the current socio-economic system of exploitation, exclusion and the destruction of the environment with a proven democratic alternative.

Cornerstone Community Housing

Location: Eugene, OR

Website: cornerstonecommunityhousing.org

A quality, dignified, and affordable home is one of the least costly and most effective ways to deliver healthcare support. Residents living in affordable housing most often have extreme socioeconomic disadvantages and a disproportionate burden of health disparities and health inequities.

 In 2015, we reconstructed our services delivery and launched Healthy Homes, a program focused specifically on health and wellness. Healthy Homes is an innovative strategy to support interventions and services that promote housing access, retention, and stabilization.

We partner with many local organizations both to ensure efficiency and ensure that residents are offered the best possible programs and services right in their own communities!

Cornerstone is developing more effective referrals, increasing access to health opportunities, promoting healthy lifestyles, and delivering health-related services in nontraditional health care settings so Lane County families can begin building strong and healthy foundations to thrive!

Council for Canadian Urbanism

Location: Canada

Website: canadianurbanism.ca

The Council for Canadian Urbanism (CanU) is a movement and organization of city planners, urban designers, architects landscape architects, engineers, developers and other urbanists operating across Canada, in urban design leadership positions within city governments and the private or community sectors.

CanU strives to connect urbanists across Canada and has actively promoted the inclusion of all regions with representation in both English and French, in the use of best practices and in sharing experience in the building of great communities.

CREATE Streets

Location: Great Britain

Website: createsteets.com

We are a RESEARCH INSTITUTE. We conduct and collate high quality research into what people actually want and what therefore drives long term value generation.

We ARGUE FOR CHANGE. We argue for specific changes to policy to make it easier to build the homes and streets that people actually want. We want homes for people not stakeholders.

We ADVISE. We are making our research available to landowners, developers, councils and Registered Social Landlords. We use our StreetScore tool to help investors, developers, councils and RSLs understand the correlations between what they own or build and happy, mixed communities for the long term.

We help DEVELOP. We are starting to identify actual sites for potential building and redevelopment and working with communities, housing associations and landowners and developers with the right long term values to help facilitate street-based development.

Creating Places for People

Location: Australia

Website: urbandesign.gov.au

This report explores how the Australian Government can work with other governments, business and the community to encourage and support walking and riding as part of the transport systems in Australia's cities and towns.

Creating Places for People is a collaborative commitment to best practice urban design in Australia. The Protocol is the result of two years of collaboration between peak community and industry organisations, states, territories, local governments, and the Australian government. The quality of our neighbourhoods, towns and cities have a significant impact on our daily lived experience. Quality urban design makes a valuable contribution to our economy, our natural and built environments, and the liveability of our cities.

It allows local business to thrive. It attracts people to visit, live and work in a location. It considers the landscape, encourages biodiversity, and incorporates natural ecosystems. It has an important influence on our physical and mental health. It provides opportunities for healthy lifestyles and community interaction.

Creative Cities Network

Location: International

Website: en.unesco.org/creative-cities

The UNESCO Creative Cities Network (UCCN) was created in 2004 to promote cooperation with and among cities that have identified creativity as a strategic factor for sustainable urban development. The 116 cities which currently make up this network work together towards a common objective: placing creativity and cultural industries at the heart of their development plans at the local level and cooperating actively at the international level.

By joining UCCN, cities commit to sharing their best practices and developing partnerships involving the public and private sectors as well as civil society in order to: strengthen the creation, production, distribution and dissemination of cultural activities, goods and services; develop hubs of creativity and innovation and broaden opportunities for creators and professionals in the cultural sector; improve access to and participation in cultural life, in particular for marginalized or vulnerable groups and individuals; fully integrate culture and creativity into sustainable development plans.

UCCN covers seven creative fields: crafts and folk arts, media arts, film, design, gastronomy, literature and music.

Cultural Landscape Foundation

Location: Nationwide

Website: tclf.org

The Cultural Landscape Foundation (TCLF) is the only not-for-profit 501(c)3 foundation in America dedicated to increasing the public's awareness and understanding of the importance and irreplaceable legacy of its cultural landscapes.

Through education, technical assistance, and outreach, we broaden awareness of and support for historic landscapes nationwide in hopes of saving this diverse and priceless heritage for future generations. While TCLF seeks donations to support its efforts, it is not a membership organization.

TCLF's overall success can be measured by the millions of people who have learned about cultural landscapes through its website, publications and events—as well as through the growing national awareness of the importance of America's cultural landscapes and the increasing efforts to document and protect this heritage.

CyArk

Location: International

Website: cyark.org

CyArk is a 501(c)3 non profit organization with the mission of: digitally preserving cultural heritage sites through collecting, archiving and providing open access to data created by laser scanning, digital modeling, and other state-of-the-art technologies. Unlike cultural artifacts safely housed in museums, cultural heritage sites are constantly at risk. They are exposed to the daily effects of the natural environment, from the seemingly benign: sun, wind, and rain; to the dramatic-earthquakes, fire, and humans.

To better understand the threats facing cultural heritage, CyArk has also developed an interactive hazard map to help visualize individual site risk. Digitally preserving these sites provides heritage professionals with tools they can use to help physically preserve their sites. Digital capture of the world's significant heritage sites ensures these places will be available for the future, while uniquely telling their story today.

CyArk uses the data captured in the creation of educational and cultural tourism media which is then broadly disseminated via the CyArk website.

Cycles of Change

Location: East (S.F.) Bay, CA

Website: cyclesofchange.org

Cycles of Change creates healthier East Bay communities by helping youth and adults gain tools for more environmentally and economically sustainable living through school-based bicycle education, job training, watershed education, and community earn-a-bike programs.

In all of our relationships, we strive to live by community agreements. Cycles' community agreements are: We are all teachers and students; we celebrate diversity in all forms; we honor and respect the present, past, and future; we are guided and inspired by love; we are guardians of each others' peace and well-being.

We aim to promote economic equity and social justice through fulfilling, valued employment and the distribution or affordable sale of needed resources. Our intent is that the value of our work is recognized by the larger community. Our goal is that all staff are secure in their monetary and non-monetary needs, and have opportunities for personal growth and creative engagement in their work.

DataCommon

Location: Southeast Florida

Website:
http://sfregionalcouncil.org/portfolio-item/data-common/

The Southeast Florida DataCommon is a unique tool that can be used to promote better communication, more informed policymaking, and broad-based collaboration around issues of shared importance.

It is a resource for grant writers; providing data and analyses of relevant community and regional trends. Information provided in the context of larger issues can further community participation and engagement to bring about positive community change. It provides a portal through which users can easily access and visualize data about Southeast Florida's communities.

A critical component the DataCommon is the importance and relevance of the information being presented to professional users, academics, policymakers, business leaders, and members of the general public. This platform was developed to encourage and facilitate meaningful dialogue within and amongst these groups. The continued development and expansion of the DataCommon will be instrumental in advancing a shared understanding of the Region and the opportunities and challenges facing our communities and fellow residents.

Data Driven Detroit

Location: Detroit, MI

Website: datadrivendetroit.org

From the Michigan Metropolitan Information Center at Wayne State University, to the Southeast Michigan Information Center at United Way, there have been many initiatives to collect and democratize data about Detroit and its neighborhoods.

Within its first year, Data Driven Detroit (D3) was selected by the National Neighborhood Indicators Partnership (NNIP). NNIP is a select group of organizations that have built advanced and continuously updated data systems to track neighborhood conditions in their cities. In December 2012, after an extensive period of review, discussion and due diligence, D3 became an affiliated program of the Michigan Nonprofit Association.

This move has strengthened D3's operations and increased our exposure to a statewide network of member nonprofits and philanthropic organizations. D3 provides accessible, high-quality information and analysis to drive informed decision-making. D3 believes that direct and practical use of data by grassroots leaders and public officials promotes thoughtful community building and effective policymaking.

Democracy Collaborative

Location: Nationwide

Website: democracycollaborative.org

Through our cutting edge research and our many diverse programs, the Democracy Collaborative works to carry out a vision of a new economic system where shared ownership and control creates more equitable and inclusive outcomes, fosters ecological sustainability, and promotes flourishing democratic and community life.

We are a national leader in equitable, inclusive and sustainable development through our Community Wealth Building Initiative. This initiative sustains a wide range of advisory, research and field building activities designed to transform the practice of community/economic development in the United States. We also host the Next System Project, ongoing intellectual work designed to connect community wealth building to the larger context of systemic economic transformation.

Our staff and associates are involved in a wide range of projects involving research, training, policy development, and community-focused work designed to promote an asset-based paradigm of economic development and increase support for transformative strategies among community stakeholders, anchor institutions, and key policymakers.

DesignAlabama

Location: Alabama

Website: designalabama.org

Our primary mission is to advocate for the collaboration of the design arts and their importance in creating and enhancing place in Alabama. DesignAlabama is a nonprofit, citizen-led organization that seeks to raise the bar for design in our great state through education of the applied arts, promoting designers who live and work in Alabama and supporting sound design thinking to sustain our communities.

DesignAlabama was founded in 1987 under the wing of the Alabama State Council on the Arts. The organization has since developed initiatives to bring awareness to design professions that help shape how we live and the environment around us. The design arts supports a range of interconnected fields including architecture, engineering, graphic design, industrial design, interior design, landscape architecture and urban design.

Some of our most impactful initiatives have been our Mayor's Design Summits. In these daylong workshops civic leaders work with designers and planners to excavate ideas that will help make their communities desirable, profitable and more livable.

Design for the Just City

Location: Nationwide

Website: designforthejustcity.org

The Just City Lab investigates the definition of urban justice and the just city and examines how design and planning contribute to the conditions of justice and injustice in cities, neighborhoods and the public realm.

Imagine that the issues of race, income, education and unemployment inequality, and the resulting segregation, isolation and fear, could be addressed by planning and designing for greater access, agency, ownership, beauty, diversity or empowerment.

Now imagine the "Just City" – the cities, neighborhoods and public spaces that thrive using a value-based approach to urban stabilization, revitalization and transformation. Imagine a set of values that would define a community's aspiration for the Just City, and imagine that we can assign metrics to measure design's impact on justice. Imagine we can use these findings to design interventions that minimizing the conditions of injustice.

Design Trust for Public Space

Location: New York, NY

Website: designtrust.org

The Design Trust for Public Space (DTPS) has improved the quality of public space and the dialogue around it in New York City, championing new ideas and nascent projects. It has broadened the definition of public space by embracing a range of sites, issues and arenas. When DTPS was founded, it stood relatively alone in its field –though not without models and precedent –to provide think-tank-like planning services focused exclusively on public space.

Much has changed since DTPS' inception. New York City has experienced the proliferation of organizations concerned with the quality of public space and design, many which have taken on similar issues and even adopted planning methodologies that follow DTPS' successful fellow model.

DTPS itself is a much different organization today than it was years ago, with paid professional staff, a professional leadership of stature, a growing board, and and a track record that has set a standard for the quality of product delivered by each project. Yet DTPS' impact and reputation are largely unknown beyond the design community.

Ecology of Absence

Location: St. Louis, MO

Website: preservationresearch.com

Ecology of Absence is a chronicle of architectural events in the St. Louis region that started as a companion to the website of the same name. The major theme of the blog is historic architecture and the primary goal is to build awareness of that architecture and the forces — social, economic, aesthetic, ecological — that create, threaten and sustain it.

The editorial approach is to "strike the roots" and look beyond threatened buildings at the larger forces that create, change and often destroy the built environment of the city. Public policy is a key part of the analysis. Consequently, the blog focuses on changes in the built environment that come about as St. Louis attempts to stem the deindustrialization, depopulation, shrinking public services and loss of architectural fabric that define the modern American urban condition. There is occasional coverage of other cities and adjacent areas in Missouri and Illinois.

Ecology of Absence welcomes guest articles. Articles will be published if relevant to the blog's focus, well-researched and well-written. Photographic and video submissions are also welcome.

Elev8

Location: Nationwide

Website: elev8kids.org

Elev8 brings together schools, families and other community partners in low-income areas — to ensure that students succeed in middle school and beyond. Part of a growing movement of community schools around the country,

Elev8 extends learning opportunities for students beyond the classroom and traditional school year, provides high-quality school-based health services to children and their families, encourages parents to be actively involved in their children's education, and offers family support and resources designed to promote economic stability, good health and continuing education.

Individually, these components play a pivotal role in children's lives. Elev8 thoughtfully integrates them because we believe an approach that considers the whole child and their family will have the greatest impact. We focus on the middle grade students because those years are a time of critical transition for young people. Elev8 aims to ensure that by the time students finish 8th grade, they are prepared for high school and go on to graduate.

EngagingCities

Location: Nationwide

Website: engagingcities.org

EngagingCities is an online magazine that shares creative strategies and new technologies to foster public engagement for livable communities.

EngagingCities is a gathering place for exploring the ideas and tools that are empowering people to become part of the creative process of planning for better communities.Our goal at Engaging Cities is simple: to inspire urban planners, architects, developers, educators, economists, and policy makers to apply new approaches and technologies in ways that make our communities more participatory, collaborative, and effective. We highlight new online tools and examine how they can be used in the emerging culture of citizen participation and engagement. We also explore low-tech, high-impact strategies for community involvement.

Every day, new projects and developments across the globe demonstrate creative ways for including citizens in the shaping of places. EngagingCities is where you can follow and become part of this movement. We think that the rise of interactive web-based technologies is going to profoundly remake our cities – large and small, across the world.

Eno Center for Transportation

Location: Nationwide

Website: enotrans.org

The Eno Center for Transportation (Eno) was founded in 1921 by William Phelps Eno (1859-1945), who pioneered the field of traffic management in the United States and Europe. Mr. Eno sought to promote safe mobility by ensuring that traffic control became an accepted role of government and traffic engineering a recognized professional discipline.

Eno focuses on all modes of transportation, with the mission of cultivating creative and visionary leadership for the sector. We pursue this mission by supporting activities in three areas: professional development programs, policy forums, and publications.

Eno is a non-profit charitable foundation, recognized by the IRS as a 501(c)(3). It is an operating foundation and does not make grants. About half of the Foundation's work is supported by its endowment; the remainder is supported by tuition and fees, contracts, and publication sales. In order to make the best use of its resources, the Foundation often works in partnership with government agencies, professional organizations, and other private organizations.

Envision Utah

Location: Utah

Website: envisionutah.org

In 1997, Envision Utah launched an unprecedented public effort aimed to keep Utah beautiful, prosperous, and neighborly for future generations. As a neutral facilitator, Envision Utah brought together residents, elected officials, developers, conservationists, business leaders, and other interested parties to make informed decisions about how we should grow. Empowering people to create the communities they want is still our goal.

To understand our neighbors' hopes for the future, Envision Utah conducted public values research, held over 200 workshops, and listened to more than 20,000 residents between 1997 and 1999. We heard a common dream: safe, close-knit communities; opportunities for our children, time to do what matters most and the security of a good job. To achieve the public's aspirations, in 1999 we created the Quality Growth Strategy, which provides voluntary, locally-implemented, market-based solutions.

Simply said, it's a strategy developed by the people of Utah to make our lives better – that provides more choices for how we, and the next generation, would like to live.

Evacuteer

Location: New Orleans, LA

Website: evacuteer.org

Evacuteer is a non-profit organization incorporated by the State of Louisiana on June 8, 2009, and approved as a 501(c)3 tax-exempt entity by the IRS in 2009. Evacuteer recruits, trains, and manages evacuation volunteers (evacuteers) who assist with New Orleans' public evacuation option called the City Assisted Evacuation Plan (CAEP).

The CAEP activates when a mandatory evacuation is called in the city of New Orleans and is designed to move 25,000-30,000 New Orleanians without transportation. The City has successfully implemented the plan once, in advance of Hurricane Gustav (Sept. 2008), when 18,000 residents utilized the CAEP.

Evacuteer is an organization created out of lessons learned from that experience. Through an existing agreement with the City of New Orleans Office of Homeland Security and Emergency Preparedness (NOHSEP), the City of New Orleans has authorized Evacuteer to manage all volunteers who work within the CAEP at 17 neighborhood pick-up points, at the Union Passenger Terminal for evacuee processing, and at City Hall to assist with hotline operation.

Families United for Racial and Economic Equality

Location: Brooklyn, NY

Website: furee.org

Families United for Racial and Economic Equality (FUREE) is a Brooklyn-based multiracial organization made up almost exclusively of women of color.

We organize low-income families to build power to change the system so that all people's work is valued and all of us have the right and economic means to decide and live out our own destinies. We use direct action, leadership development, community organizing, civic engagement and political education to win the changes our members seek. Our guiding principle is that those directly affected by the policies we are seeking to change should lead the organization.

FUREE has engaged over 3,000 local area residents, allies to work towards addressing the negative impacts of market-led development that effectively displaced many low-income and working class families and small businesses while limiting access to basic support services our families need to break the cycle of poverty. This member-led campaign has won two court battles against eminent domain.

Flint Public Art Project

Location: Flint, MI

Website: flintpublicartproject.com

We organize workshops and temporary installations to inspire residents to reimagine the city, reclaim vacant and underutilized buildings and lots, and use innovative tools to steer Flint's long-range planning.

We support collaboration among local residents and organizations as well as with leading artists, architects, planners and community organizers from around the world, connecting Flint to regional, national and global movements to revitalize neighborhoods and cities through art and design.

We will document and amplify the many ways local residents, businesses and institutions are transforming Flint and its public image and identity, and will broadcast this new story to audiences throughout the city and the world.

Focus Maui Nui

Location: Maui, HI

Website: focusmauinui.com

Focus Maui Nui is a community process seeking the input of local citizens in a discussion about what residents want for the future of our islands (Maui, Molokai, Lanai, and Kahoolawe) which together make up Maui Nui and Maui County.

The project is designed to bring individuals, organizations, and communities throughout the county together to identify and prioritize shared values and to send clear messages to local leaders about what we want for our islands, our communities, and our future.

In summer 2003, Focus Maui Nui brought together a diverse cross-section of nearly 1,700 residents to discuss their values and priorities. Over three months, 167 small group discussions took place in neighborhood homes, churches, shopping centers and workplaces, with each group ultimately developing a list of key strategies that could shape Maui's future.

Community leaders have pledged to uphold the findings of this process and to make decisions based on the vision that emerges.

Food Trust

Location: Philadelphia, PA

Website: thefoodtrust.org

The Food Trust is an offshoot of Philadelphia's venerable Reading Terminal Market. It began with one farmers' market at Tasker Homes, a public housing development in South Philadelphia. Once a week, with the help of the Tasker Homes Tenant Council, we set up one long table overflowing with produce. It was the only source of fresh fruits and vegetables in the community. "People hadn't seen that kind of quality produce in their neighborhood before," The Food Trust founder Duane Perry recalls.

In the two decades since the opening of the Tasker Homes market, The Food Trust has worked with neighborhoods, schools, grocers, farmers and policymakers in Philadelphia and across the country to change how we all think about healthy food and to increase its availability.

Together, we've brought supermarkets to communities that have gone decades without one. We've helped corner store owners introduce fresh produce, low-fat dairy and whole grains. We've taken soda and junk food out of schools, and we've taught students to appreciate foods like apples and cherry tomatoes.

French Quarter Citizens

Location: New Orleans, LA

Website: frenchquartercitizens.org

French Quarter Citizens (FCQ) was founded in 1994 to strengthen the quality of residential life in the French Quarter. Not surprisingly, we focus much of our effort in this area. FQC is heavily engaged in the current efforts to write a new ordinance to control noise; we insist on simple, straightforward, and easily enforced rules that protect and promote the music — not noise — for which New Orleans is justly famous. Cleanliness and sanitation has declined recently.

FQC is helping lead an effort to identify and propose solutions to the challenges of keeping the French Quarter clean, having the trash collected on time, and reducing the number of trash containers littering our sidewalks.

Other quality of life issues occupying our efforts and members include supporting the eradication of graffiti, promoting neighborhood consensus making Cabrini Park better for dogs and humans, strengthening controls on filming in the Quarter, making changes in parking regulations to favor residents, and getting the city to crack down on illegal short-term rentals that undermine the Quarter's residential values.

Fresh, Local and Equitable

Location: Nationwide

Website: kresge.org/freshlo

Fresh, Local and Equitable (FreshLo) grantees across the country are developing innovative approaches to economic development, cultural expression and health through food-oriented development.

In 2017, the Kresge Foundation granted $4.6 million to communities to implement projects.

Each organization completed a one-year planning phase to address the needs of their community and engage residents in the design of the project in order to receive implementation funding.

Fresh Moves

Location: Chicago, IL

Website: freshmoves.org

Step inside a reconditioned city bus in Chicago this Thanksgiving, and you can buy cranberries and green beans where commuters once sat. The Fresh Moves mobile produce market-- which inspired other pop-up grocery stores across the country-- plans to reopen on the weekend of November 23, intent on proving to larger supermarkets that there's a market for fresh produce in food deserts.

Steven Casey, who first founded Fresh Moves with a single recycled city bus in 2011 agrees that access isn't the only critical factor. "If you've been without healthy food for so long, you might not necessarily know what to do if someone sells you that food today. There's an education or re-education process, I believe, [that] is a strong component of what we need," Casey says, explaining that Fresh Moves provides cooking demos and recipe cards.

Casey says he still believes "access is equally important and just because a store might look relatively close on a map doesn't mean it's easy to get there."

Friends of the River

Location: California

Website: friendsoftheriver.org

We have always see-sawed between periods of drought and extreme precipitation that can lead to biblical flooding in California. Climate change is making these shifts increasingly severe. Relying on 20th century thinking, like building new dams, simply doesn't work anymore. We built a vast network of more than 1,400 dams over the last century. Building more would do very little to reduce flood risk or increase water supply, but it would add billions of dollars of debt for the next generation and destroy rivers. We can't dam our way to paradise.

We must protect our remaining free flowing rivers and advance innovative water solutions that are more environmentally sound, economically efficient and yield meaningful amounts of water for all Californians.

To ensure a safe and reliable water system that protects communities and the rivers that flow through them FOR launched our Point Positive campaign to promote innovative, 21st century water solutions that diversify our water system and work with nature instead of against it.

Friends of the Riverfront

Location: PIttsburgh, PA

Website: friendsoftheriverfront.org

The Three Rivers Heritage Trail is a wonderful pedestrian trail and greenway system in the Pittsburgh region running for 24 miles along both sides of the Allegheny, Monongahela and Ohio Rivers. It is an almost complete public route for cyclists, walkers, runners, and in some places rollerbladers.

The Friends of the Riverfront (FOTR) was established for the creation and continued expansion of the Three Rivers Heritage Trail. We advocate for and build multi-use trails, parks and continuous public access along our three rivers through active partnerships with communities, public leaders, citizens and organizations from around the region.

As FOTR continues to push for the development of the few remaining "missing links" in the trail system in the City of Pittsburgh, we have started to engage adjacent municipalities along the Allegheny, Monongahela and Ohio Rivers in an effort to establish regional connections and generate economic opportunities and environmental regeneration in smaller riverfront towns.

Friends of the Urban Forest

Location: San Francisco, CA

Website: fuf.net

Friends of the Urban Forest's (FUF) mission is to promote a larger, healthier urban forest as part of San Francisco's green infrastructure through community planting, tree care, education, and advocacy. Each year, FUF helps communities plant nearly 1,000 trees.

Neighbors organize the plantings. FUF obtains permits, removes sidewalk concrete, supplies tools and materials and selects, purchases and delivers the trees. On planting day, FUF volunteers work side-by-side with residents. After the work is done, everyone celebrates over a community lunch. At plantings neighbors meet-often for the first time-to improve their streetscape. Spirits are high and everyone has a good time for the common good.

In 1995, FUF formally instituted Tree Care to improve tree health and to increase survival rates. Friends of the Urban Forest's certified arborists, assisted by volunteers and trainees, prune and restake existing street trees.

Fund For Democratic Communities

Location: Southeast U.S.

Website: f4dc.org

The Fund for Democratic Communities (F4DC) was founded in 2007 and since then has made over $1 million in grants to support grassroots democratic organizing efforts, primarily focused in the Southeastern United States. We operate with a strong belief in the power of ordinary people in neighborhoods, workplaces and other communities to understand and solve their own problems when given an opportunity to put their heads together and hear the diverse voices of all involved.

The F4DC, is a Greensboro, North Carolina based private foundation that supports community-based initiatives and institutions that foster authentic democracy to make communities better places to live.

F4DC makes grants to groups that engage in participatory democracy to further their social change objectives; convenes groups and individuals committed to social and economic justice through deepening democratic practice, conducts research, and produces materials to nurture the growth of authentic democracy.

Global Designing Cities Initiative

Location: International

Website: globaldesigningcities.org

The Global Designing Cities Initiative is a program of the National Association of City Transportation Officials, a New York-based, 501(c)3, non-profit organization.

Our mission is to inspire a shift toward safe, sustainable, and healthy cities through transforming our streets.

We are a team of designers, planners, and urban strategists committed to working in support of city practitioners to get projects on the ground. We focus on empowering local officials and communities to become changemakers, equipping them with the knowledge, tools, and tactics needed to improve urban mobility and fundamentally change the role of streets in our cities.

Our work is informed by the strategies and international best practice captured in the Global Street Design Guide.

Greater Places

Location: Nationwide

Website: greaterplaces.com

GreaterPlaces is a virtual planning assistant for creating great places, cities & towns:

We provide all aspects of city/town design under one "digital roof" with the intention of sharing the information you need on fast-moving technology and trends to stay ahead. We strive to provide connections with civic innovators: planners, engineers, architects, elected officials, and more. We aggregate tools to better organize, visualize & share ideas with clients & the community and for professionals, a powerful new marketing tool to get in front of clients.

We provide a bi-weekly newsletter. If you need something that's not here, send us a message using the "Send Ideas or Questions" section. As a small business, the ability to affordably get in front of customers in new ways gives the business owner an advantage

Great Rivers Greenway

Location: St. Louis region

Website: greatriversgreenway.org

There is a place that has always been wireless, cordless and decidedly "unvirtual" — Nature. Great Rivers Greenway has been preserving nature just for you. Greenways give you somewhere to go, close to home, when you feel a deep longing for time away from a screen.

Listen to a bird song you've never heard before. Smell the foliage in bloom. See your very first river otter and witness what nature can do for you. Great Rivers Greenway District is the public organization leading the development of the region-wide system of high-quality greenways, parks and trails known as The River Ring. Our mission is to make St. Louis a better place to live while creating an enduring legacy for future generations.

Working with our many partners, the development of The River Ring and its greenways represents a common cause with common ground.

Clean air, clean water, healthy forests, connected neighborhoods and walkable streets provide a healthier lifestyle which serves as a catalyst for economic vitality, making the St. Louis region a better place to live.

Greenbelt Alliance

Location: SF Bay Area, CA

Website: greenbelt.org

We help create great cities and neighborhoods – healthy places where people can walk and bike, communities with parks and shops, transportation options, and homes that are affordable. Together these amazing places drive the Bay Area's economic vitality and quality of life.

We work both regionally and locally, blending expertise with on-the-ground action to help people explore our great region, make their neighborhoods thrive and save treasured landscapes from sprawl. The places that make the Bay Area special are incredibly diverse, which is why Greenbelt Alliance's work takes many forms, from saving farms in Santa Clara County and wildlife habitat in Sonoma County to revitalizing commercial strips in Silicon Valley and Oakland.

At Greenbelt Alliance, we bring people together around the places that matter to them. We envision a future where the Bay Area's natural and agricultural landscapes that provide so much are protected and nurtured.

Greenlining Institute

Location: Nationwide

Website: greenlining.org

Founded in 1993, The Greenlining Institute is a policy, research, organizing, and leadership institute working for racial and economic justice. We work on a variety of major policy issues, from the economy to environmental policy, health care and many others, because we recognize that economic opportunity doesn't operate in a vacuum.

Headquartered in California, Greenlining's approach focuses on bringing grassroots community leaders face to face with leading public and private sector leaders. We design and support policies designed to open doors to opportunity. We don't see these interactions as a zero-sum game in which one side must win and the other must lose. Instead, we reach for win-win solutions that expand the size of the pie for all Americans.

Our Leadership Academy trains the leaders of the future to be effective advocates for justice and fairness. Driving everything we do is a vision of equity in which the American Dream is truly within reach of all.

Grow Smart Rhode Island

Location: Rhode Island

Website: growsmartri.org

Grow Smart Rhode Island (GSRI) is a 501 (c)3 nonprofit organization that advocates sustainable economic growth that builds upon and strengthens Rhode Island's exceptional quality of place. GSRI grew out of a 1997 conference that attracted 600 concerned citizens and representatives from organizations and agencies working on the issue of sustainable economic growth, urban revitalization and quality of place in Rhode Island.

Discussions prompted by the conference identified the need for a flexible but focused organization to link these groups and educate citizens, business leaders and elected officials about the impacts of urban disinvestment and the loss of open space in our more rural areas and about state and local policies and strategies to combat these trends.

In the 14 years since our founding, GSRI has developed a broad and powerful coalition that includes business and religious leaders, university presidents, builders, realtors, farmers, historic preservationists, environmentalists, affordable housing experts, municipal planners and others.

Healthy Rowhouse Project

Location: Philadelphia, PA

Website: healthyrowhouse.org

Founded in 2014, The Healthy Rowhouse Project (HRP) is a growing coalition of organizations in the fields of health, housing, planning and preservation dedicated to improving substandard conditions and health in rowhouses owned by lower-income Philadelphians.

The HRP is funded by the Oak Foundation. Twenty Philadelphia leaders have joined the Advisory Committee. They are lending their expertise to recommend comprehensive Healthy Rowhouse policy, design, construction, and financing tools to assist rowhouse owners to improve their housing quality. Philadelphia rowhouses are an extraordinary asset that allows the city to offer homeownership to a higher share of low-income households than almost any city in the country.

Philadelphia's rowhouses, an affordable, energy-efficient and durable form of housing, make up 70% of all homes in the city. Homeowners include 78% of Philadelphians over age 60. In addition, rowhouses provide homes for approximately 40% of all renters.

Homes For All

Location: Nationwide

Website: homesforall.org

Homes For All (HFA) is a national campaign with the goal of broadening the conversation of the housing crisis beyond foreclosure and putting forth a comprehensive housing agenda that also speaks to issues affecting public housing residents, homeless families, and the growing number of renters in American cities.

HFA aims to protect, defend, and expand housing that is truly affordable and dignified for low-income and very low-income communities by engaging those most directly impacted by this crisis through local and national organizing, winning strong local policies that protect renters and homeowners, and shifting the national debate on housing.

HFA is working collaboratively across sectors to develop national housing policy that ensures that our communities and future generations have homes that are truly affordable, stable, and dignified. Today, people who buy their homes are thrown out if they cannot make their mortgage payments, renters are either the new hot deal on the housing market or dealing with rising rents and costs and buildings in disrepair.

Hope in Shadows

Location: Vancouver, BC

Website: hopeinshadows.com

Hope in Shadows (HIS) is an innovative community engagement project that creates positive and meaningful interactions between residents from Vancouver's Downtown Eastside and people from other neighbourhoods in the Lower Mainland and beyond. Each year, winning photos from the HIS photography contest are featured in a calendar that local residents can sell on the street through our vendor program.

HIS demonstrates that meaningful employment opportunities positively contribute to the well-being and dignity of people impacted by poverty and marginalization.

Each year we distribute 200 disposable cameras to residents of the Downtown Eastside as part of a photo competition that gives residents the chance to document their own community. Forty photographs are chosen for exhibition, and 12 make it into the HIS calendar. In 2013, we piloted a second photography contest in North Vancouver. After attending a basic sales training session, low-income residents are licensed to sell the HIS calendar on the streets of Vancouver.

Idea Village

Location: New Orleans, LA

Website: ideavillage.org

In 2000, The Idea Village was formed by a group of New Orleans citizens who believed entrepreneurship is a catalyst for positive change. The Idea Village formalized in 2002 as an independent 501c3 nonprofit organization with a mission to identify, support, and retain entrepreneurial talent in New Orleans by providing direct service to high-impact entrepreneurs, educating the broader community, and supporting initiatives that strengthen our entrepreneurial infrastructure.

From 2009-2014, The Idea Village provided direct support to over 3,411 New Orleans entrepreneurs by engaging over 2,600 professionals to allocate 68,543 consulting hours and $2.5 million in seed capital.

The Idea Village hosts New Orleans Entrepreneur Week, a business festival that has become the platform for the New Orleans entrepreneurial ecosystem. We work hard in the company of entrepreneurs, mentors, investors, and professionals who are committed to helping local startups launch.

[im]possible living

Location: International

Website: blog.impossibleliving.com

Abandoned buildings are everywhere: in city centers, suburbs, countrysides, mountains, seasides–everywhere! They are left there, day after day, night after night. They don't scream, they don't bleed, they just lose a little piece everyday, so you don't really realize that a certain place is falling down, until one day it's impossible to recover it and the only thing that is left to do is tear it down!!

How is our society managing these buildings? Most of the time just ignoring them, preferring to leave them behind and build new buildings instead! This approach is cheaper in the short term, but definitely it is not in the long run.

There is an enormous power trapped in these ruins and [im]possible living is a project that aims to free this power up. It won't be easy, but we want to try to reverse this trend and give a new life to these places.

Indego

Location: Philadelphia, PA

Website: rideindego.com

The City of Philadelphia, with funding from the William Penn Foundation, added 30 additional stations to connect underserved communities with parks, waterways and resources throughout Philadelphia. The City of Philadelphia launched Indego in 2015 as the newest form of public transportation. With more than 1000 self-service bikes and more than 105 stations, Indego offers 24/7 access to the city on your schedule. Indego is an initiative of the City of Philadelphia and sponsored by Independence Blue Cross.

Indego was launched with a strategic focus on making a bike share that is accessible and equitable to all Philadelphians, and is the lead partner of the Better Bike Share Partnership, a collaboration funded by The JPB Foundation to build equitable and replicable bike share systems.

The Better Bike Share partnership supported the City of Philadelphia's equity goals for Indego when the system launched in 2015, including the placement of 19 Indego stations in underserved neighborhoods, the industry's first integrated cash payment option, and outreach and education work in partnership with the Bicycle Coalition of Greater Philadelphia.

Innovative Housing Institute

Location: Nationwide

Website: inhousing.org

The Innovative Housing Institute (IHI) promotes providing quality affordable housing in communities throughout the nation, primarily through the policies and practices known as "inclusionary housing".

The IHI offers a great depth of knowledge and experience in the variety of inclusionary housing tools and strategies used in different local jurisdictions and states.

Inclusionary housing, also known as "inclusionary zoning", calls for a portion of housing units in residential projects to be available for low- and moderate-income households.

Many programs provide developers with "cost offsets" or incentives, such as density bonuses, zoning or design flexibility, parking reductions, fee waivers, or an expedited review process for providing these affordable units. The term inclusionary is used to counter exclusionary practices that require minimum lot sizes and setbacks, effectively preventing affordable housing from being built.

Institute for Local Self Reliance

Location: Nationwide

Website: ilsr.org

The Institute for Self Reliance's (ISLR) mission is to provide innovative strategies, working models and timely information to support environmentally sound and equitable community development. To this end, ILSR works with citizens, activists, policymakers and entrepreneurs to design systems, policies and enterprises that meet local or regional needs, to maximize human, material, natural and financial resources and to ensure that the benefits of these systems and resources accrue to all local citizens.

Since 1974, ILSR has championed local self-reliance, a strategy that underscores the need for humanly scaled institutions and economies and the widest possible distribution of ownership.

ILSR challenges the view that localism and regionalism represent a misguided desire to turn back time.

ILSR challenges the conventional wisdom that bigger is better, that separating the producer from the consumer, the banker from the depositor and lender, the worker from the owner is an inevitable outcome of modern economic development.

Institute for Public Architecture

Location: Nationwide

Website: instituteforpublicarchitecture.org

The Institute for Public Architecture (IPA) promotes socially engaged architecture through urban research projects and a future residency program for design practitioners. By supporting architects and allied professionals working in the public interest, the IPA strives to improve our public realm.

IPA envisions a world where architects and allied professionals are provided the resources and support they need to create excellent work in the public interest and to contribute to the high quality design of the public realm.

IPA believes that supporting and elevating the profile of architects working in the public interest is the first step to creating better design for traditionally underserved populations. We believe that a vibrant network of 'activist' architects is critical to the improvement of design in the public realm. We believe that high quality design in the public realm is critical to the production of socially equitable environments.

Intelligent Community Forum

Location: International

Website: intelligentcommunity.org

"Intelligent communities" are those which have – whether through crisis or foresight – come to understand the enormous challenges of the broadband economy, and have taken conscious steps to create an economy capable of prospering in it.

They are not necessarily big cities or famous technology hubs. They are located in developing nations as well as industrialized ones, suburbs as well as cities, the hinterland as well as the coast.

The good news is that, while the broadband economy presents an epic challenge to communities, it also hands them a powerful new competitive tool. Beginning in the 1990s, carriers deployed the local networks that most of us think of as "broadband" – DSL, cable, satellite and wireless – within neighborhoods, towns and cities.

Interise

Location: Nationwide

Website: interise.org

What started as a single class of 14 business owners in 2004 has grown into a national network of thriving small businesses, community development organizations, government agencies, anchor institutions, instructors, and business experts. We envision an economy that works for all, where the playing field is level, knowledge is shared, and everyone gets a seat at the table. We build trust, and put people and relationships before profit or transactions.

Interise licenses our Streetwise 'MBA' to partners who deliver it through their own locally branded programs. Delivered by our partners, our capacity-building Streetwise 'MBA' provides small business owners with the knowledge, know-how, and networks they need to achieve scale.

Our research and evaluation agenda focuses on existing small businesses in low and moderate income communities, business networks, and community resilience. By studying the complex systems that influence small business success in lower income communities, our research examines trends in growth opportunities, financing, and barriers to scaling small business.

In The Public Interest

Location: Nationwide

Website: inthepublicinterest.org

In the Public Interest (ITPA)is a comprehensive resource center on privatization and responsible contracting. It is committed to equipping citizens, public officials, advocacy groups, and researchers with the information, ideas, and other resources they need to ensure that public contracts with private entities are transparent, fair, well-managed, and effectively monitored, and that those contracts meet the long-term needs of communities.

The mission of the ITPA is to provide: accurate, high-quality information, across a variety of sectors and jurisdictions about trends and developments in privatization, the impacts of privatization on the public, and responsible contracting policies and practices.

We also provide tools and resources to help public officials, researchers, advocates, workers, and administrators ensure that essential public goods and services are available to those who need them, managed by people who are publicly accountable, and affordable to all.

ioby

Location: Nationwide

Website: ioby.org

"It's our backyard, and it belongs to us and our kids." –Brandon Whitney

It started with a legacy of city dwellers. These people—your everyday neighbors—created daily change. They cleaned up lots, planted trees and gardens and brought fresh produce to areas that needed it. They got their hands dirty, but few noticed. Joyful as it was, the change was tiny—and isolated. To gain steam, it needed power, money, people and hype. It needed a platform.

Enter ioby. ioby connects change with resources. It enables all of us to invest in change—then see (and live with) the return on our investment. There are everyday neighbors taking small steps—bringing sunlight, open space, fresh food and greenery into our backyards.

ioby is an environmental nonprofit organization. Our name is derived from the opposite of NIMBY (it's our backyard). We have a mission to deepen civic engagement in cities by connecting individuals directly to community-led, neighbor-funded environmental projects in their neighborhoods.

Jane's Walk

Location: Toronto, Ontario

Website: janeswalk.org

Jane's Walk celebrates the ideas and legacy of urbanist Jane Jacobs by getting people out exploring their neighbourhoods and meeting their neighbours. Free walking tours held on the first weekend of May each year are led by locals who want to create a space for residents to talk about what matters to them in the places they live and work.

The main Jane's Walk event takes place annually on the first weekend of May, to coincide with Jane Jacobs' birthday. Jane's Walks can be organized and offered any other time of the year by enthusiastic local people or organizations. Jane's Walk often takes Jacobs' ideas to communities unfamiliar with her ideas, in order to advance local engagement with contemporary urban planning practices. The walks helps knit people together into a strong and resourceful community, instilling belonging and encouraging civic leadership.

Walks are led by individuals and small groups. Some are focused around historical themes more than geographical areas. Some strolls have been built around ideas.

Joint Center for Political and Economic Studies

Location: Nationwide

Website: jointcenter.org

The Joint Center for Political and Economic Studies (JCPES) works to inform and illuminate the nation's major public policy debates through research, analysis, and information dissemination, with the goal of improving the socioeconomic status of African Americans and other people of color, expanding their effective participation in the political and public policy arenas, and promoting communications and relationships across racial and ethnic lines to strengthen the nation's pluralistic society.

Our high quality research, distinctive analyses of the issues, and experience in assembling effective coalitions have been cited by policy makers as helping to generate innovative, practical solutions to America's most challenging problems.

The JCPES approach includes identifying critical and emerging issues and developing research parameters, as well as collaborating with well-known scholars and experts in designing and conducting rigorous investigations, studies, and reports. Our research findings are published in relevant policy circles and among targeted audiences.

Know Your Place

Location: England

Website: kypwest.org.uk

Know Your Place (KYP) is a digital heritage mapping resource to help you to explore your neighbourhood online through historic maps, collections and linked information.

KYP provides unprecedented online access to a range of historic data, but more importantly provides a place where users can add information about your local area, building a rich and diverse community map of local heritage for everyone. Its free to use and anyone can add to the map.

Know Your Place – West of England was a project which ran from June 2015 to July 2017 to expand coverage from Bristol to the six surrounding counties of Bath & North East Somerset, Gloucestershire, North Somerset, Somerset, South Gloucestershire and Wiltshire.

As part of a later extension to the project the county of Devon has now been added. This expands the coverage for the West of England by another 2,590 square miles. KYP now spans eight counties and 7279 square miles, with other counties around the UK interested in putting their areas on the map in future.

LA2050

Location: Los Angeles, CA

Website: la2050.org

LA2050 unites citizens, stakeholders, and organizations to address our region's toughest challenges. LA2050 is rooted in a vision of a successful Los Angeles—a healthy, thriving, and desirable place to live.

LA2050 looks at the health of the region as it exists today along eight well-defined indicators: education, income & employment, housing, public safety, health, environmental quality, social connectedness, and arts & cultural vitality. We've made informed projections about where we'll be in the year 2050 if we continue on this current path.

The condition of Los Angeles today matters because who we are and how we live now sets us on a course for who we will be and how we will live tomorrow. We are confident that with your help, we will shape the LA story anew – and build the LA2050 of our aspirations.

Explore LA2050.

Landmarks Association of St. Louis

Location: St. Louis, MO

Website: landmarks-stl.org

St. Louis, bequeathed with a wealth of historically and architecturally significant buildings, owes the conservation and adaptive reuse of much of that inheritance to Landmarks Association of St. Louis, Inc.

Organized in 1958 and incorporated as a non-profit in 1959, Landmarks is the primary advocate for the region's built environment. In the early 1970's, Landmarks embarked on an ambitious citywide survey to identify important sites and potential historic districts.

The survey pace accelerated in the late 1970s when the federal government passed legislation offering tax credits for renovating properties listed on the National Register of Historic Places. By the mid 1980s St. Louis led the country in historic tax credit reinvestment, thanks in large part to Landmarks' nominations to the Register. Landmarks also played a key role in framing Missouri's historic rehab tax credit program in 1997.

Laws That Shaped L.A.

Location: Los Angeles, CA

Website: kcet.org/laws-that-shaped-la

For more than a year now, the 'Laws That Shaped L.A.' column has been chronicling a running list of laws that a range of experts say have made a significant impact on the people and places of this region -- and oftentimes, far beyond.

As regular readers of the column know, the columns are automatically archived.

That automatic archive appears chronologically by the date each column was published.

League to Save Lake Tahoe

Location: Lake Tahoe, CA and NV

Website: keeptahoeblue.org

The League to Save Lake Tahoe (LSLT) is dedicated to protecting, restoring, and advocating for the ecosystem health and scenic beauty of the Lake Tahoe Basin. The organization focuses on water quality and its clarity for the preservation of a pristine Lake for future generations.

The LSLT is a solutions-based environmental watchdog. Our core focus is to protect Lake Tahoe's inspiring water clarity, We advocate for strong environmental regulation and enforcement to protect Lake Tahoe for this and future generations and collaborate with stakeholders to address environmental issues.

LSLT supports collaborative, innovative, and science-based solutions to environmental issues facing the Lake.

Legacy Cities Initiative

Location: Nationwide

Website: legacycities.org

The Legacy Cities Initiative (LCI) aims to establish a framework for the revitalization of legacy cities, improve the community of practice working on these issues, and change the policies that govern practice in these cities.

Th LCI was founded by The American Assembly, the J. Max Bond Center on Design for the Just City, and the Center for Community Progress.

LCI believes that these cities can thrive once again if the assets, energy, capacity and love for these places at the local level can be nurtured by effective shifts in public policy, coordinated advocacy, mutual learning about what works, and careful, strategic implementation.

Levitt Foundation

Location: Nationwide

Website: levitt.org

The Levitt program is transformative. Abandoned, blighted places: whether a neglected and gang-infested park, a dormant downtown, a vacant lot or a toxic brownfield—are today vibrant, welcoming destinations where families, friends and people of all ages and backgrounds gather to discover new worlds, and each other, through free, live music.

Levitt's free concerts, easily accessible locations and open lawn settings foster social interactions among people of all ages and backgrounds — strengthening the social fabric of our cities. There's no front row, no back row, just a grassy open lawn filled with friends dancing, children playing and neighbors picnicking. Levitt venues are places where people relax and enjoy the company of others. Where we embrace our shared humanity.

Levitt concerts feature first-rate, critically acclaimed artists free of charge. This enables people from all walks of life—many of whom could not afford the cost of a concert for themselves or their families—to have those meaningful cultural experiences essential to a healthy, happy life.

Livable Berkeley

Location: Berkeley, CA

Website: liveableberkeley.org

Livable Berkeley is a coalition of citizens, environmental leaders, social equity advocates, design professionals, city planners and progressive builders who seek to build upon Berkeley's renowned commitment to environmental stewardship, economic justice and social responsibility.

We look forward to engaging our neighbors and coalition partners as we bring to fruition the changes and improvements in store for Downtown Berkeley. With the city as a financial partner, Berkeley can join the "Open Streets" movement along with 70 other cities in the U.S., bringing the long-term community benefits of this exciting event to Berkeley.

Sunday Streets (also called "Open Streets") closed streets to automobile traffic for a day so that people may use the space for just about any activity other than driving. The streets become parks as foot traffic replaces car traffic. People bike, jog and dance, meet up with friends, meet someone new, and play.

Living Cities

Location: Nationwide

Website: livingcities.org

Living Cities harnesses the collective power of philanthropy and financial institutions to improve the lives of low-income people and the cities where they live. Living Cities' core values – those we believe are fundamental to the organization's success in achieving its mission – are collaboration, innovation, leadership, and impact.

These organizational values guide our everyday decisions about how, why and what we do. As a partnership of foundations and financial institutions, collaboration is core to who we are. We believe that respect, diverse perspectives and the open exchange of ideas will lead to the innovative solutions and catalytic change that our country needs.

We take risks, catalyze fresh thinking, and test new approaches in order to creatively disrupt the status quo, change broken systems and provide opportunities for all. We continually ask difficult questions, challenge obsolete norms, and support others in their efforts to do the same. We look for strategic opportunities to promote our point of view and to move innovation from the periphery to the mainstream.

Local Bites

Location: Fresno, CA

Website: tastefresno.com/localbites

Local Bites is a partnership between TasteFresno and Mayor Swearengin to encourage Fresnans to support locally owned restaurants—it's a simple, yet effective way that we can all have an impact on our local economy!

Once a month, Mayor Swearengin will dine out at a local restaurant (on her own dime, of course!).

You're invited to join, or create your own Local Bites night—to participate, simply make the commitment to dine locally about once a month.

(this program is not currently functioning)

Local Initiatives Support Corporation

Location: Nationwide

Website: lsic.org

Founded in late 1979, Local Initiatives Support Corporation (LISC) is the largest community development support organization in the country. For almost three decades, LISC has connected local organizations and community leaders with resources to revitalize neighborhoods and improve quality of life.

The LISC model assembles private and public resources and directs it to locally-defined priorities. Our unique structure enables local organizations to access national resources and expertise and our funding partners to leverage their investment and achieve an impact that is truly remarkable.

LISC is dedicated to helping community residents transform distressed neighborhoods into healthy and sustainable communities of choice and opportunity — good places to work, do business and raise children. LISC mobilizes corporate, government and philanthropic support to provide local community development organizations with loans, grants and equity investments as well as local, statewide and national policy support technical and management assistance,

Long Island Index

Location: Long Island, NY

Website: longislandindex.org

The Index is a project of the Rauch Foundation, a Long Island-based family foundation established in 1961. The Foundation acts as the convener of the Long Island Index Advisory Committee and the financial underwriter of the Index. In 2011, the Long Island Press described the Index as "the most definitive status report on the quality of Long Island life.

Long Island is one region with a shared history, geography, beaches, aquifers, and a shared future. But from day- to-day, our differences seem more apparent than our similarities. We are 2 counties, 2 cities, 13 towns, 95 incorporated villages, 37 legislative districts. We have 110 library districts, 125 school districts and 187 fire districts plus hundreds of other special districts. Sometimes it is easier to see these as many fragments rather than our shared whole.

We created The Long Island Index to focus on our region as a whole – those things that unite us, issues that can only be understood by looking at the big picture.

Los Angeles Conservancy

Location: Los Angeles, CA

Website: laconservancy.org

The Los Angeles Conservancy (LAC) is a nonprofit membership organization that works through education and advocacy to recognize, preserve, and revitalize the historic architectural and cultural resources of Los Angeles County. A small group of concerned citizens formed the LAC in 1978 as part of a community-based effort to prevent demolition of the Los Angeles Central Library, built in 1926.

The LAC now has more than 6,000 members and hundreds of volunteers, making it the largest local preservation group in the U.S. With a mandate of awareness, assistance, and action, the Conservancy works to preserve historic resources by developing preservation and reuse strategies, as well as raising awareness of their value in strengthening communities, conserving resources, fostering economic development, and enriching lives.

The LAC's advocacy efforts have helped to save and revitalize such beloved landmarks as the former Cathedral of St. Vibiana, the Wilshire May Company Building, the Wiltern Theatre, the Cinerama Dome, Frank Lloyd Wright's Ennis House, and the world's oldest remaining McDonald's restaurant.

Los Angeles Forum for Architecture and Urban Design

Location: Los Angeles, CA

Website: laforum.org

Founded in January of 1987, the Los Angeles Forum for Architecture and Urban Design (LAFAUD) has organized lecture series and site visits to significant buildings and sites throughout Los Angeles and the region. We have hosted a number of special events, symposia and a theory reading group; held several design competitions; distributed a quarterly newsletter and online articles; produced many publications, as well as national-distributed pamphlet-sized books.

LAFAUD provides a framework for design professionals and members of the general public to explore, evaluate, and impact the development of architecture in Los Angeles.

The Forum seeks to reach out beyond the confines of professional organizations, schools and established groups and does not limit itself to one approach to design or theory. It provokes discussion, seeks out places and designs unseen or unnoticed by the general public, publicizes architectural investigation and commentary.

Los Angeles Nomadic Division

Location: Los Angeles, CA

Website: nomadicdivision.org

Los Angeles Nomadic Division (LAND) is a non-profit organization founded in 2009 committed to curating site-specific public art exhibitions in Los Angeles and beyond.

LAND believes that all people deserve the opportunity to experience innovative contemporary art in their everyday existence, to enhance their quality of life and ways of thinking about their community. In turn, artists deserve the opportunity to realize projects in the public realm, unsupported through traditional institutions.

LAND brings contemporary art outside of the walls of museums and galleries, into our shared public spaces and unique sites, in Los Angeles and beyond. LAND supports dynamic and unconventional artistic practices using a tripartite approach: commissioning public projects of site- and situation-specific works with national and international contemporary artists, and collaborating with a variety of institutions and organizations, such as universities, museums, and theaters as well as other types of spaces, industries, and entities.

Lowell Plan

Location: Lowell, MA

Website: lowellplan.org

The Lowell Plan, Inc. was established as a nonprofit economic development organization in 1980. For 30 years, the Lowell Plan has sustained constructive and productive dialogue among the city's key leaders in business, government, education, and community development. In its simplest terms, the answer is that Lowell's public and private leaders have maintained an ongoing dialogue that has yielded practical responses to the challenges and opportunities facing the city.

The formula sounds simple, but it was revolutionary at the outset. The Lowell Plan created a neutral ground where public and private sector officials could speak candidly and collaborate on priority issues. Through the years the names and faces have changed, but the board's structure and reputation for getting results ensure that the pieces keep coming together month after month.

Going forward, the Lowell Plan is committed to fostering a dialogue that will take Lowell well into the 21st century as a city with a productive and sustainable economy; lifelong educational opportunities and vibrant and diverse cultural offerings.

Machine Project

Location: Los Angeles, CA

Website: machineproject.com

Machine Project is a storefront space in the Echo Park neighborhood of Los Angeles that hosts events about all kinds of things we find interesting – scientific talks, poetry readings, musical performances, competitions, group naps, cheese tastings and so forth. We usually do about two events a week, open to the general public and free of charge. Usually at 8pm. Information on upcoming events can be found on our page.

Machine Project is an informal educational institution located in the same storefront space as mentioned above. We teach all kinds of things we find interesting – electronics, sewing, pickling, computer programming, car theft and so forth. We usually have one or two class going a week, open to the public for a fee by pre-registration. Information on upcoming classes can be found on our classes page.

Machine Project is a loose group of artist/performer collaborators, who do projects together when invited by other people and institutions, usually museums. Information on special projects can be found on our projects page.

Main Street Alliance

Location: Nationwide

Website: mainstreetalliance.org

Main Street Alliance (MSA) is a national network of small business coalitions working to build a new voice for small businesses on important public policy issues. Alliance small business owners share a vision of public policies that work for business owners, our employees, and the communities we serve.

MSA is national network formed in 2008 to give Main Street small business owners a new voice in the health care reform debate, and has since broadened its focus to work on a range of issues that matter to small businesses and local economies. Our growing network includes small business coalitions in over a dozen states.

MSA is directed by a National Steering Committee of small business leaders from our state coalitions. The National Steering Committee identifies issue priorities, establishes MSA policy positions, and provides strategic direction and guidance for our work. MSA creates opportunities for small business owners to speak for ourselves on issues that impact the health and well-being of our businesses, employees, and communities.

Main Street America

Location: Nationwide

Website: mainstreet.org

Over the past 30 years, the Main Street movement has transformed the way communities think about the revitalization and management of their downtowns and neighborhood commercial districts. Cities and towns across the nation have come to see that a prosperous, sustainable community is only as healthy as its core.

Specifically, Main Street is three things: a proven strategy for revitalization, a powerful network of linked communities, and a national support program that leads the field. The Main Street Four-Point Approach is a unique preservation-based economic development tool that enables communities to revitalize downtown and neighborhood business districts by leveraging local assets - from historic, cultural, and architectural resources to local enterprises and community pride. It is a comprehensive strategy that addresses the variety of issues and problems that challenge traditional commercial districts.

Main Street is a national movement that has spanned three decades and taken root in more than 2,000 communities.

Mannahhata 2409

Location: New York, NY

Website: mannahatta2409.blogspot.com

Mannahatta 2409, currently under development, will offer an online forum to enable the public to develop and share climate-resilient designs for Manhattan based on realistic model assessments of carbon, water, biodiversity, and population.

Because ecology has largely been ignored by past generations, New York City, like most modern cities, has inherited a series of interconnected problems of ecological performance: stormwater management, climate change adaptation and mitigation, brownfield remediation, and ecological restoration.

The first step in rectifying these problems is to think of the city as a vital ecological place, an ecosystem with attributes like a forest, a wetland, or a stream, but designed for people.

Mannahatta 2409 will be a map-based web application meant to inspire, inform, and generate new ideas about sustainable urban forms from the many diverse people who love New York City, Manhattan in particular.

Mayors' Institute on City Design

Location: Nationwide

Website: micd.org

The Mayors' Institute on City Design (MICD) is a leadership initiative of the National Endowment for the Arts in partnership with the American Architectural Foundation and the United States Conference of Mayors, with support from United Technologies. Since 1986, MICD has helped transform communities through design by preparing mayors to be the chief urban designers of their cities.

MICD achieves its mission by organizing sessions where mayors engage leading design experts to find solutions to the most critical urban design challenges facing their cities. Sessions are organized around case-study problems. Each mayor presents a problem from his or her city and gets feedback from other mayors and design experts.

Every year, the partner organizations plan and manage six to eight Institute sessions held throughout the country. Each two and one-half day session is limited to less than twenty participants, (half mayors and half a resource team) consisting of outstanding city design and development professionals.

Meeting of the Minds

Location: International

Website: cityminded.org

Meeting of the Minds (MOTM) is a global knowledge sharing platform based in San Francisco, CA. Since it was founded, MOTM has been dedicated to a singular proposition: bring together a carefully chosen set of key urban sustainability and technology stakeholders and gather them around a common platform in ways that help build lasting alliances.

MOTM focuses on the innovators and initiatives at the bleeding edge of urban sustainability and connected technology. Through our blog, magazine, webinars, monthly meetups, workshops, roundtables, and an annual summit held each fall, we invite international leaders from the public, private, non-profit, academic and philanthropic sectors to identify innovations that can be scaled, replicated and transferred from city-to-city and across sectors.

Among the thousands of international leaders who participate in the MOTM network are innovators scaling-up practical urban solutions in infrastructure, policy, design, equity, technology, energy, mobility, water, finance, and more.

Metamorphosis

Location: Los Angeles, CA

Website: metamorph.org

Our mission is to understand the transformation of urban community under the forces of globalization, new communication technologies, and population diversity so that our research can inform practitioner and policy maker decisions. Our site of study is Los Angeles and its many ethnic communities of both new and settled immigrants.

We have developed a communication infrastructure perspective that privileges a grassroots understanding of how people construct and revitalize their residential communities, and how they go about solving everyday problems of family, health, inter-group relations, and ethnic identity. Our challenge is to make the communication infrastructure of daily life visible so that it can be employed by residents, practitioners, and policy makers to improve the quality of family and community life.

At the heart of this infrastructure is the neighborhood storytelling network. This network involves residents, community organizations, and geo-ethnic media in a dynamic communication process.

Metrominuto app

Location: Pontevedra, Spain

Website: metrominuto.info

The city of Pontevedra in northwest Spain has become a leader in walker-friendly urban policy over the past 15 years. In light of its relative anonymity and population of 83,000, one might find it difficult to imagine the traffic congestion that prompted this transformation. However, as the capital of its province, county and municipality, Pontevedra attracted enough automobile commuters each day to overwhelm its antiquated streets.

Instead of razing old buildings and constructing bigger roads, the city council began taking proactive measures to reduce traffic. They widened sidewalks, established a free bike-lending service, installed speed bumps and set a speed limit of 30 kilometers per hour throughout the city. They even banned motorized transport in sections of Pontevedra. Walking zones now extend from the historic center to streets and squares in newer neighborhoods.

Although the driving ban initially faced resistance, it is now broadly supported and has become an essential part of the city's identity as an attractive place to live. To further improve walkability, Pontevedra's city council produced a map that visualizes the distances and travel times between key places on foot at an average speed of five kilometers per hour.

Meu Rio

Location: Rio de Janeiro, Brazil

Website: meurio.org.br

Meu Rio ("My Rio" in Portuguese) is an independent popular movement for and by the people of Rio de Janeiro, Brazil.

MY RIO meurio.org.br – This is our headquarter site, where you can enroll in our missions and receive instructions on the next goals to transform Rio de Janeiro. You are also located inside of everything that My Rio is doing on the streets, the large network and in our other tools. Want to be a change agent in Rio de Janeiro?

PRESSURE COOKER paneladepressao.org.br – In the Pressure Cooker, population and social movements can create their own campaigns of popular pressure. Because all the pressure is faster. The recipe is simple: you point to a problem, call other people who want the same change directly and press politicians, businessmen and public officials, by email, Twitter or Facebook.

TRUTH OR DARE verdadeouconsequencia.org.br
Know the game Truth or Dare? In these elections, we created a way for you to find your ideal councilman and candidate to know what people expect from a good politician. After, Truth or Dare will get you to the polls to vote.

Midtown Detroit, Inc.

Location: Detroit, MI

Website: midtowndetroitinc.org

Midtown Detroit, Inc. (MDI) is a nonprofit 501(c)(3) organization created to support and enhance community and economic development in the Midtown area through collaboration and partnerships with key stakeholders and supportive funders. MDI is the result of a collaborative merger between the University Cultural Center Association and the New Center Council, whose organizations had a similar mission and a focus on real estate development, economic development, and the preservation of the districts' history.

Both prior organizations have been responsible for a remarkable number of successful community initiatives that have encouraged new housing development, increased visitorship to area attractions, supported new and increased commercial activity, and expedited infrastructure improvements to revitalize the greater Midtown district.

Midtown's revitalization has been successful due to collaboration and committed participation of the area's arts, culture, academic, medical and service institutions, corporations, government, property and business owners and community and neighborhood organizations.

151

Mile High Connects

Location: Denver,CO

Website: milehighconnects.org

Quality health care, good jobs and top schools are at the foundation of a vibrant life. And yet, for many in our community a lack of public transit can limit their access to these important resources. Mile High Connects (MHC) wants to change that. MHC is committed to ensuring that existing and future transit service by RTD, including the FasTracks expansion, and enabling all people to connect to the opportunities that can lead to a more affordable and better quality life.

MHC will help ensure that public transit links people to the places they live, work, learn and play in a safe, convenient and affordable manner. The mission is to ensure that the Metro Denver regional transit system fosters communities that offer all residents the opportunity for a high quality of life.

MHC will realize this vision by: increasing resources to build affordable, inclusive communities along the transit system, influencing policy to ensure that all people are involved and considered in urban and economic planning and increasing resident engagement in neighborhoods directly affected by the expanding transit system.

MillionTreesNYC

Location: New York, NY

Website: milliontreesnyc.org

MillionTreesNYC, one of the 132 PlaNYC initiatives, is a citywide, public-private program with an ambitious goal-to plant and care for one million new trees across the City's five boroughs over the next decade. By planting one million trees, New York City can increase its urban forest—our most valuable environmental asset made up of street trees, park trees, and trees on public, private and commercial land—by an astounding 20%, while achieving the many quality-of-life benefits that come with planting trees.

The City of New York will plant 70% of trees in parks and other public spaces. The other 30% will come from private organizations, homeowners, and community organizations. Trees enrich and improve our environment and dramatically increase the overall quality of life in New York City. Our urban forest totals over 5 million trees and 168 species.

It can be found throughout the city along streets, highways, in neighborhood playgrounds, backyards, community gardens, and even along commercial developments. There are 6,000 acres of woodlands in parks alone!

Mount Vernon Triangle CID

Location: Washington,D.C.

Website: mountvernontriangle.org

The Mount Vernon Triangle Community Improvement District (MVTIC) is a private, nonprofit organization established to enhance the overall quality of life for residents, visitors, employees, and property owners in Washington DC's newest 24-hour neighborhood by providing a clean and safe environment, marketing, and fostering planning and economic development.

The vision for the MVTCID is to develop Mount Vernon Triangle as a new neighborhood on the east end of Downtown DC with new residences, Class-A offices, and fine places to shop, dine, and enjoy this vibrant mixed-use community that is active day and night. A Community Improvement District is a designated geographic area in which the property owners have agreed to pay a supplementary real property tax in order to raise funds for designated programs or projects, such as to augment street cleaning services provided by the City.

Under District law, the MVTCID is legally defined as a Business Improvement District.

Movement for Black Lives

Location: Nationwide

Website: m4bl.net

We know that black people have always made a way, even when the odds were against us – as they are now. An administration full of racist, sexist, fear mongers are moving into the White House – and we should all be concerned about their potential impact on our lives.

We are just beginning to see the effects of the fear and violence they support. Recently we've seen an increase in hate crimes and hate speech against black people, the vandalizing of black churches, and vigilantes taking up arms in our communities to incite violence and fear. In the face of all this, millions of black folks across the country are asking, "What can we do?"

We are confident that we have the commitment, the people power and the vision to organize our country into a safe place for Black people — one based on inclusivity and justice, not intimidation and fear. Join us. Our vision has always included our children living in safety, our communities having control of our destinies, and an economy that provides good jobs, food, clean water and safe housing for our people. That hasn't changed, and if anything, this moment requires that we work even harder for those things.

Municipal Art Society

Location: New York, NY

Website: mas.org

The Municipal Art Society (MAS) is New York's leading organization dedicated to creating a more livable city. For 120 years, MAS—a nonprofit membership organization—has been committed to promoting New York City's economic vitality, cultural vibrancy, environmental sustainability and social diversity.

Working to protect the best of New York's existing landscape, from landmarks and historic districts to public open spaces, MAS encourages visionary design, planning and architecture that promote resilience and the livability of New York. Founded in 1893, the MAS has helped create a more livable city by advocating for the quality of the built environment through excellence in urban planning, design, preservation and placemaking through the arts. From saving Grand Central Terminal and the lights of Times Square to establishing groundbreaking land-use and preservation laws that have become national models,

MAS is at the forefront of New York's most important campaigns to promote our city's economic vitality, cultural vibrancy, environmental sustainability and social diversity.

National Low Income Housing Coalition

Location: Nationwide

Website: nlihc.org

In 1974, Cushing N. Dolbeare founded the Ad Hoc Low Income Housing Coalition in response to the Nixon administration's moratorium on federal housing programs. While this group focused on federal advocacy, other members established the Low Income Housing Information Service (LIHIS) in 1975 to provide information on housing problems and federal housing programs, as well as technical assistance and support to state and local housing advocacy efforts.

In 1978, the ad hoc coalition was incorporated as the National Low Income Housing Coalition (NLIHC). The two organizations operated jointly, with LIHIS focusing on information, public education, and technical assistance, and NLIHC focusing on advocacy. LIHIS launched a major initiative in 1992 to strengthen partner housing coalitions at the state level in response to devolution of many federal programs.

The maturation of NLIHC and LIHIS led to a decision in 1996 to formally merge the two organizations into one 501(c)(3) membership organization, governed by one board of directors.

National Performance Network

Location: Nationwide

Website: npnweb.org

The National Performance Network (NPN) is a national organization supporting artists in the creation and touring of contemporary performing and visual arts. NPN is about community engagement, touring, creating, as well as sharing ideas and knowledge. NPN is about representing all artists who create something new and supporting the presenters who take the risk in showcasing it.

NPN has brought innovative performing artists to all corners of the United States for more than 25 years. Begun in 1985 by David White at Dance Theatre Workshop in New York, NPN was founded to address the issues of artistic isolation and the economic constraints of moving art around the country and the sharing of artistic and community voices. From a beginning of 14 organizations as "primary sponsors," the network now numbers 61,

In 2007 the Visual Artists Network (VAN) began as a pilot program and was formally launched with the selection of 15 VAN Partners that are leading contemporary arts organizations from across the United States.

Nature of Cities

Location: International

Website: thenatureofcities.org

The mission of The Nature of Cities (TNOC) is to promote worldwide dialog and action to create green cities that are sustainable, resilient, livable, and just. The TNOC community comprises a broad diversity of people, from architects and designers to scientists, from practitioners to entrepreneurs and artists pursuing transformational dialog that leads to the creation of better cities for all.

TNOC is a virtual magazine and discussion site on cities as ecosystems. It is a global collective of contributors, an essay, long-form, media, and discussion site devoted to cities as social-ecological spaces, ecosystems of people, buildings, open spaces, and nature. We believe that cities are human habitat, and that design with nature and public open space at the metaphorical center is key to urban resilience, sustainability, livability and justice.

Cities are fundamentally ecological spaces. They are ecosystems packed with trees and vegetation that comprise an urban forest. They house birds, insects, small mammals, diverse ecological habitats, and more.

Nature Sacred

Location: Washington, DC area

Website: naturesacred.org

In an increasingly urbanized world, we are bound to find a better connection with ourselves in nature than with our WiFi networks. Cities, in a counterintuitive way, are more sustainable settlements that provide housing for thousands or millions of people, as high-density centers offer energy efficient smaller homes, transit systems, and concentrations of services. Yet life in cities can be stressful, and residents can feel removed from nature, the wellspring of all that sustains us.

Research of the past few decades provides evidence of how nearby nature is essential for human habitat. Nature offers restorative settings and experiences, including sacred encounters. A luminous sunset or a glimpse of the tracery of tree branches are just a few of the nature encounters that can instill a sense of calm, contemplation, or inspiration.

The mission of the TKF Foundation is to provide the opportunity for a deeper human experience by inspiring and supporting the creation of public greenspaces that offer temporary sanctuary, encourage reflection, provide solace and engender peace and well being.

Nature Vancouver

Location: Vancouver, BC

Website: naturevancouver.ca

Nature Vancouver is a not-for-profit charitable society registered under the BC Societies Act. Membership in the Society is open to all. The Society is a Federated Club of BC Nature. The Society is organized into a number of sections; birding, botany, conservation, geology, marine biology and photography.

The Society holds regular evening meetings and invites guest speakers to make presentations on natural history topics. These meetings are open to the general public, with no admission fee, and are held from January to April; and from September to November. In addition, the birding, botany and marine biology sections sponsor monthly meetings from January to April and September to December. The conservation section also meets monthly.

The Society publishes *Discovery,* a journal of natural history. It is published twice a year and is distributed to all members of the Society. *Discovery* is also available to non-members by subscription. The Society also publishes a quarterly newsletter, *Vancouver Naturalist,* which contains the details of the Society's programs and events.

Neighborhood Assistance Corporation of America

Location: Nationwide

Website: naca.com

The Neighborhood Assistance Corporation of America (NACA) is a non-profit, community advocacy and homeownership organization. NACA's primary goal is to build strong, healthy neighborhoods in urban and rural areas nationwide through affordable homeownership.

NACA has made the dream of homeownership a reality for thousands of working people by counseling them honestly and effectively, enabling even those with poor credit to purchase a home or modify their predatory loan with far better terms than those provided even in the prime market.

NACA has a tremendous track record of successful advocacy against predatory and discriminatory lenders as well as providing the best mortgage program in America with $10 billion in funding commitments. NACA is the largest housing services organization in the country and is rapidly expanding.

Neighborhood Story Project

Location: New Orleans, LA

Website: neighborhoodstoryproject.org

In 2004, the Neighborhood Story Project (NSP) was founded as a book-making project based in the neighborhoods where we live and work. We work with writers in neighborhoods around New Orleans to create books about their communities.

The NSP started at our neighborhood public school, John McDonogh Senior High, with the idea of our students investigating their worlds. For a year, the students wrote, photographed, interviewed and edited. In 2005, we brought out five books (collaborative ethnographies) about New Orleans.

In the years since, NSP has expanded our practice of collaborative ethnography outside of schools, producing books and posters that do the work of telling stories of the city. We work with authors and neighborhoods, then celebrate publication with block parties. The books have gone on to be citywide bestsellers, selling more than 35,000 books. We continue the work as a center at the University of New Orleans, with Rachel in the Department of Anthropology, and Abram in the College of Education and Human Performance, and publish our books through UNO Press and our own 501(c)3 non-profit.

Neighborland

Location: New Orleans, LA

Website: neighborland.com

Neighborland is a new way to shape the development of your city. It's a tool for learning more about your neighborhood and having a say in its future.

We started this project with a simple question: "What if residents could easily share their ideas for improving their neighborhoods?" Could these ideas help community leaders, entrepreneurs, and developers better meet the needs their communities? Can presenting this data in a transparent and friendly way help shape the development of a neighborhood — or at the very least, provide a new form of public accountability?

Take a look around the site and you'll see neighbors sharing ideas and asking (and answering) questions about their communities. You can listen to neighbors you're interested in and receive notifications to keep track of the ideas that you care about. We believe sketching an idea that might benefit your neighborhood is a meaningful civic action, and with Neighborland you don't need to go to a city council meeting or be friends with a developer to do it. We're working hard to make sure your ideas are seen by the right people.

NeighborWorks America

Location: Nationwide

Website: neighborworks.org

We are an organization that cares deeply about affordable housing and community development and the people who benefit from them. Their safety and wellbeing is why we come to work in the morning and why we put in long hours and years of service.

To be successful at this work, there is simply no substitute for the reach, breadth and know-how of the NeighborWorks network – more than 240 of the nation's best community development organizations – and the support structure that we have built over more than 35 years.

We build the skills, supplement the resources and amplify the reach of these organizations so they can build more houses, empower more individuals and transform more communities than they would be able to do on their own.

New Amsterdam Market

Location: New York, NY

Website: newamsterdammarket.org

New Amsterdam Market is a reinvention of the "public market", once a prevalent institution in the City of New York. Revived for our present times and needs, New Amsterdam Market will incubate a new and growing economic sector: small businesses such as butchers, grocers, mongers, and other vendors who source, produce, distribute, and sell foods made with regional ingredients as well as carefully selected imports. We are also reintroducing and developing the concept of market fare prepared with regional, seasonal ingredients.

Our vision is to revive the historic Fulton Fish Market, a priceless public legacy that is owned by the people of New York and whose two market sheds have remained empty and unused since 2005. By bringing residents back to the Seaport, we are reviving the East River Market District - a rare fragment of our city's first port and oldest commercial neighborhood as a thriving, public destination for all New Yorkers.

We envision the Fulton Fish Market redeveloped as a permanent, year-round, wholesale and retail distribution center dedicated to responsible agriculture, regional sourcing, and fair trade.

Nextdoor

Location: Nationwide

Website: nextdoor.com

Nextdoor is the private social network for you, your neighbors and your community. It's the easiest way for you and your neighbors to talk online and make all of your lives better in the real world. And it's free. We're a team of 46 people who are passionate about building stronger and safer neighborhoods. We're based in San Francisco, California.

Thousands of neighborhoods are already using Nextdoor to build happier, safer places to call home.

Nextdoor's mission is to bring back a sense of community to the neighborhood, one of the most important communities in each of our lives. We created this company because we believe that the neighborhood is one of the most important and useful communities in a person's life. We hope that neighbors everywhere will use the Nextdoor platform to build stronger and safer neighborhoods around the world.

We believe technology is a powerful tool for making neighborhoods stronger, safer places to call home.

nextSTL

Location: St. Louis, MO

Website: nextstl.com

First launched in 2004 as urbanSTL, nextSTL has become the preeminent online hub for those wanting to know more about the St. Louis community.

The blog has been recognized for feature articles discussing changes and issues critical to the continuing resurgence of the City of Saint Louis and the Metro Area.

The forum has emerged as the go-to source for issues current and critical to St. Louis, with more than 2,700 registered users, 7,000 total topics and more than 176,000 posts. Forum topics have frequently featured breaking news and have been sourced by multiple news outlets.

Northeast Los Angeles Riverfront Collaborative

Location: Los Angeles, CA

Website: mylariver.org

The Northeast Los Angeles Riverfront Collaborative (NELA RC) is an innovative, interdisciplinary partnership that will capture the energy of the Los Angeles River as a catalyst for implementing revitalization strategies and help NELA communities to thrive.

The NELA RC process builds upon the growing momentum of efforts already underway to transform the river, and aims to create a riverfront district as a focal point of community revitalization, recreational activities, environmental stewardship, sustainable civic engagement, and economic growth for the entire city.

What do you want your L.A. River to be?

Oakland Community Land Trust

Location: Oakland, CA

Website: oakclt.org

Oakland Community Land Trust (OakCLT) promotes neighborhood stability and community involvement through the provision of permanently affordable housing and access to land. OakCLT also supports the development of open space, agricultural, commercial, and retail facilities that serve low-income residents.

We strive to foster leadership through a responsible and informed board of community members and serve as a platform to empower low-income residents of Oakland.

A community land trust is a nonprofit organization that acquires and stewards land in trust for the permanent benefit of low-income communities. This community-controlled land can be put to a wide variety of uses, including homeownership, rental, and cooperative housing, food production through community gardens and urban agriculture, commercial space, and more. Community land trusts take a long view of community change and development. CLTs seek to ensure that our cities permanently support equitable housing opportunities and access to land for low-income residents.

Ohio & Erie Canalway Coalition

Location: Pennsylvania and Ohio

Website: ohioeriecanal.org

The Ohio & Erie Canal opened up the frontier settlement of Ohio and provided settlers with a reliable form of transportation to ship products. This unique waterway is being rediscovered as communities seek to celebrate their heritage while stimulating community and economic development. Today, there is renewed interest in the preservation, development and interpretation along the resources of the Ohio & Erie Canal as it extends from New Philadelphia to Cleveland.

Established in 1989, Ohio & Erie Canalway Coalition is a private, non-profit organization working on the development of the Ohio & Erie National Heritage Canalway. The Coalition provides educational programs, events and publications about the Heritage Canalway while developing strong working relationships with partners to preserve and interpret the natural, historical and recreational resources throughout the corridor.

Canalway represents a biological mosaic with natural systems of forests, bogs, marshes, streams and lakes that are interspersed with cities, towns and villages, orchards, and croplands.

Old North Saint Louis Restoration Group

Location: St. Louis, MO

Website: onsl.org

Old North Saint Louis Restoration Group is pursuing a comprehensive revitalization strategy rooted in the community's vision of a sustainable and welcoming neighborhood that offers high quality housing opportunities for a diverse population from all walks of life.

What's New in Old North (an article in the *St. Louis Magazine*) chronicles the dramatic transformation under way in the neighborhood of Old North St. Louis.

As a neighborhood just north of Downtown St. Louis, Old North is becoming a dynamic urban village of new and historic homes, a landmark eating establishment, beautiful community gardens, and a diverse, friendly, and engaged community.

On The Commons

Location: Nationwide

Website: onthecommons.org

On the Commons (OTC) is a commons movement strategy center founded in 2001. Our purpose is to activate the emergence of a commons-based society by building and bringing visibility to the commons movement, initiating and catalyzing commons work that focuses on commons-based solutions and developing and encouraging commons leadership.

OTC has initiated successful co-creative projects and innovative strategies for protecting our essential common, such as water, food, farmland, and seeds; showcased commons-based solutions on a local and national level; and inspired commons activists to make a difference in their communities and the world.

OTC believes it is possible to remember, imagine, and create a society that goes beyond the constructs and confines of individual ownership. To work on the commons is to work to enliven the deep and ancient memory we all hold of egalitarian and reciprocal relationship, of belonging, of authentic community, and of love, wonder, and respect for the natural world.

OpenCity Projects

Location: Toronto

Website: opencityprojects.com

Launched in 2006, Open City Projects is a creative lab that is all about great urban experiences. We aim to elevate the role of public space in building strong communities through our research, community engagement and blog.

In our research projects, we view "place" through the eyes of people who use it every day and apply our insights to help create a vibrant urban experience. Our blog covers creative uses of public space in cities around the world—from sustainable materials and beautiful landscaping to unexpected programming.

The OpenCity name was inspired by Toronto. Now in its 'youth', we feel that Toronto is open like no other city—open to change, cultures and interpretation. We take inspiration from this open quality and learn from other cities' design approach to inform our creative perspective.

OpenOakland

Location: Oakland, CA

Website: openoakland.org

OpenOakland, a Code for America Brigade, is a civic innovation organization that brings together coders, designers, data geeks, journalists, and city staff to collaborate on solutions to improve how our local government serves all citizens of Oakland.

We draw on our wide range of expertise and perspectives to build open-source applications and working relationships that promote civic innovation and open government in Oakland.

Our projects range from events like City Camp to Open Government Pledge, to a community-based open-data portal and OaklandWiki, to apps that help you chart crime trends, submit FOIA requests and adopt your local storm drain.

Open Streets Project

Location: United States and Canada

Website: openstreetsproject.org

The Open Streets Project (OSP) is a collaboration between the Alliance for Biking and Walking and The Street Plans Collaborative.

The goal of the project is to share information about open streets and increase the number, size, and frequency of initiatives occurring across North America.

OSP began in early 2010, when Street Plans began examining the breadth and diversity of open streets initiatives in the United States and Canada. In the fall of 2010, Street Plans teamed with the Alliance with the goal of reaching local advocates and open streets organizers across North America.

OSP includes a published guide and an interactive website, which allows advocates and new open streets organizers to explore open streets efforts in other peer cities.

It also allows seasoned open streets organizers to continually update and share best practices, maps, photos, videos, and publicity materials via the individual initiative blog feature.

Operation Comeback

Location: New Orleans, LA

Website: prcno.org/programs/operation-comeback

The Preservation Resource Center's Operation Comeback promotes the purchase, renovation and sale of vacant historic properties. Started in 1987, as a focused effort to revitalize the Lower Garden District, Operation Comeback rapidly expanded and now works with dozens of neighborhood associations and community development corporations citywide.

By acquiring and renovating blighted and adjudicated properties that most would consider hopeless, Operation Comeback provides homes for first-time and repeat home buyers, serving as a catalyst for the rebirth of New Orleans' historic neighborhoods. In the effort to put as many properties back into the hands of families as possible,

Operation Comeback has developed several ways for many to become involved. The OC Revolving Fund and the Adopt a House program allow individuals, organizations, foundations and corporations to aid in the renovation or construction of homes through donations, volunteering, and education.

Opportunity Detroit

Location: Detroit, MI

Website: opportunitydetroit.com

Detroit's urban core is bursting with new businesses providing a plethora of opportunities for professionals to work downtown. Work in a fast-paced environment that inspires productivity and growth!

Come spend a little time in Detroit to discover how easy it is to find good eats, good entertainment and good times! Downtown is home to the Tigers, the Lions, the Pistons and the Red Wings and three lively casinos to try your luck. The vibrant streetscape offers hundreds of restaurants, bars, hotels, theater venues and a growing array of retail shops. Campus Martius and Cadillac Square provide year-round attractions and activities. Upcoming projects will provide more exciting new things to do as well as updated green space and artistic décor.

The urban energy and residential options in and around downtown Detroit are growing. There are more than 3,000 downtown units, and the influx of new residents is spurring new renovation projects. The city offers historical and architecturally charming buildings with a blend of renovated conveniences. One of the best things about renting and owning in and around downtown is the affordability.

Opportunity Finance Network

Location: Nationwide

Website: opportunityfinance.net

Opportunity Finance Network (OFN) is a national network of community development financial institutions (CDFIs) investing in opportunities that benefit low-income, low-wealth, and other disadvantaged communities across America. OFN members are performance-oriented, responsible investors that finance community businesses, sparking job growth in the areas that need it most, and delivering both sound financial returns and real changes for people and communities.

OFN has originated more than $23.2 billion in financing in urban, rural, and native communities through 2009. With cumulative net charge-off rates of less than 1.4%, we have demonstrated our ability to lend prudently and productively in unconventional markets often overlooked by conventional financial institutions.

CDFIs are private financial institutions that are 100 percent dedicated to delivering responsible, affordable lending to help low-income, low-wealth, and other disadvantaged people and communities join the economic mainstream.

Our Equitable Future

Location: Chicago, IL

Website: metroplanning.org/roadmap

Chicago's segregation is inextricably linked to racism. To break this cycle, our path forward must be rooted in racial equity. Doing so will unlock the potential of all the region's residents and communities. In 2015, the Metropolitan Planning Council launched a groundbreaking study to calculate the economic costs of segregation. With the Urban Institute, we documented the extreme price we pay to live so separately by race and income.

Our study revealed this singular truth: as residents of the Chicago region, our fate is shared, and by living so separately we pay a steep cost that can be measured in lost income, lost lives and lost potential. These findings have been a catalyst for meaningful action, bringing together people from diverse communities and sectors to develop solutions that will lead to a more and equitable and thriving Chicago region.

The number of government, community and business leaders who are taking action to make our region more equitable and inclusive is growing larger every day.

Our Miami

Location: Miami, FL

Website: ourmiami.org

Our Miami is a project of The Miami Foundation (TMF) developed in association with an important three-year study called Soul of the Community. Funded by the John S. and James L. Knight Foundation, Soul of the Community surveyed residents of metropolitan Miami (and 25 other cities nationwide) to explore and understand what residents like most about where they live and which factors play the biggest roles in connecting people to their place.

To evaluate these qualities in greater depth, TMF partnered with the Metropolitan Center at Florida International University. FIU gathered data in each category to better understand the degree of alignment and/or variance between Miamians perceptions and reality. TMF asked, "What can we do to make our place, our city more attractive to an increasingly mobile and global society?

Armed with powerful new data, TMF and its partners will use Our Miami to explore how Miamians can make improvements that will nurture a stronger sense of community and advance the quality of life for all area residents.

Over-the-Rhine Foundation

Location: Cincinnati, OH

Website: otrfoundation.org

The Over-the-Rhine Foundation (OTRF) is a non-profit organization, founded in 1992, to help preserve and revitalize Cincinnati's most historic, diverse and architecturally rich community.

OTRF works to preserve, protect and celebrate Over-the-Rhine, (the historic heart of Cincinnati) by encouraging community growth, sound planning and responsible, sustainable development. Over-the-Rhine will become an economic and cultural asset for the city of Cincinnati; a revitalized, safe, diverse, beautiful and vibrant community in which to live, work and play.

OTRF has been working to improve this historically significant neighborhood since 1992. We believe that Over-the-Rhine is more than simply a community worth preserving. It is the heart of Cincinnati and the key to a better future, not only for OTR - but for the region as well. OTRF embraces our mission to preserve, protect and celebrate Over-the-Rhine by creating an ecologically sustainable, urban community. We work in collaboration with like-minded organizations, dedicated to re-inventing Over-the Rhine as an exemplary, diverse neighborhood in which to live, work and play.

182

ParkScore

Location: Nationwide

Website: parkscore.tpl.org

ParkScore is the most comprehensive rating system ever developed to measure how well the 40 largest U.S. cities are meeting the need for parks.

Using an advanced GIS (Geographic Information System), ParkScore provides in-depth data to guide local park improvement efforts. Our mapping technology identifies which neighborhoods and demographics are underserved by parks and how many people are able to reach a park within a ten-minute walk. Cities can earn a maximum ParkScore of 100. For easy comparison and at-a-glance assessment, each city is also given a rating of zero to five park benches.

Parks are important to communities. Close-to-home opportunities to exercise and experience nature are essential for our physical and mental well-being. Studies show that parks can encourage physical activity, reduce crime, revitalize local economies, and help bring neighborhoods together.

PARK(ing) Day

Location: Nationwide

Website: facebook.com/PARKing-Day

PARK(ing) Day is a annual open-source global event where citizens, artists and activists collaborate to temporarily transform metered parking spaces into "PARK(ing)" temporary public places.

The project began in 2005 when Rebar, a San Francisco art and design studio, converted a single metered parking space into a temporary public park in downtown San Francisco.

Since 2005, PARK(ing) Day has evolved into a global movement, with organizations and individuals (operating independently of Rebar but following an established set of guidelines) creating new forms of temporary public space in urban contexts around the world. The mission of PARK(ing) Day is to call attention to the need for more urban open space, to generate critical debate around how public space is created and allocated, and to improve the quality of urban human habitat ... at least until the meter runs out! The PARK(ing) project was created to explore the the range of possible activities for this short-term lease, and to provoke a critical examination of the values that generate the form of urban public space.

Pennsylvania Humanities Council

Location: Pennsylvania

Website: pahumanities.org

Pennsylvania Humanities Council (PHC) programs and grants focus on areas of need where the humanities can have the greatest impact in Pennsylvania today.

PHC works with communities to build their capacity to achieve long-term goals, from engaging teens in strengthening skills for school and life, to coaching residents as they plan a better future for their town. We travel across the commonwealth and across sectors through partnerships to achieve the greatest impact and broadest reach possible. We advocate for the crucial role the humanities play in our lives and our society and for continued resources to keep them vital and visible.

An investment in the humanities is an investment in the future of our state—and our nation. The humanities can provide a path to more productive lives and increased social mobility, from engaging residents in actions that strengthen their communities, to narrowing the achievement gap among Pennsylvania's youth.

People St.

Location: Los Angeles, CA

Website: peoplest.lacity.org

People St. offers communities within the City of Los Angeles the opportunity to transform underused areas of LA's largest public asset – our 6,500 miles of city streets – into active, accessible public space. Community organizations, business owners and other groups can apply for opportunities to enhance the quality of the public realm through installing three innovative design treatments – plazas, parklets and bike corrals.

This website is your one stop shop for information, resources and materials on People St. and the process for applying to bring these projects to your neighborhood. Building from lessons learned from the city's first six pilot projects, LADOT has been working closely in an unprecedented collaboration with community members, elected officials, and other city staff to develop People St into a program that will expedite project development and implementation with a clear, consistent process.

People St. facilitates partnerships between the community and the City of Los Angeles to implement projects that transform redundant or underused areas of street into high-quality public space.

Philadelphia Parks Alliance

Location: Philadelphia, PA

Website: philaparks.org

The mission of the Philadelphia Parks Alliance (PPA) is to champion the public's interest in outstanding parks, recreation and open spaces. This is the key to making Philadelphia a healthy, vibrant and sustainable city for all.

PPA's vision of a great city is one with great parks and interconnected green spaces. PPA leads the diverse and expanding citizens' movement which shapes public policies required to build the city's premier parks and recreation system.

PPA will strive to become a primary advocate and information resource for parks and open space in our city. We are committed to building a strong and unified parks and open space coalition that will advocate for all citizens.

We will endeavor to create strategic and collaborative alliances with government and with organizations that care about our parks and open space.

Pit Stop

Location: San Francisco, CA

Website: sfpublicworks.wixisite.com/pitstop

San Francisco Public Works operates the Pit Stop program, which provides clean and safe public toilets, sinks, used needle receptacles and dog waste stations in San Francisco's most impacted neighborhoods.

The program utilizes both portable toilets, which are trucked to and from the sites daily after overnight servicing at a remote location, and the semi-permanent JCDecaux self-cleaning toilets.

All the Pit Stop facilities are staffed by paid attendants who help ensure that the toilets are well maintained and used for their intended purpose. The program, which began in 2014, now operates at 11 locations, providing an alternative to using our streets and sidewalks as a toilet. Not only do the people who need a bathroom benefit, but so do the neighborhoods.

Places

Location: International

Website: placesjournal.org

Places is an interdisciplinary journal of contemporary architecture, landscape and urbanism, with a particular focus on the public realm as both physical place and social ideal.

We publish essays, peer-reviewed scholarship, observations, reviews, visual portfolios, and occasionally poetry and fiction, with new articles appearing weekly. Whatever the format, we are dedicated to advancing public awareness of the expansive value of design research and practice, with the ultimate goal of promoting sustainable cities and healthy landscapes.

Places Journal is a 501(c)3 organization, published by the Places Journal Foundation in collaboration with the Design Observer Group. We are grateful for the support of a network of North American and European universities as well as organizational and individual sponsors.

Prior to moving online in 2009, Places was a print journal founded in 1983 by faculty at MIT and Berkeley. The entire print archive is available in pdf format.

Planting Justice

Location: East (S.F.) Bay, CA

Website: plantingjustice.org

We work to address the structural inequalities that have become embedded in our industrialized food system: the systemic exploitation of food system workers (especially undocumented farm and kitchen workers) the lack of access to fresh, nutritious food in low-income communities of color and our culture's over-reliance on packaged, processed food that is killing our bodies and our environment.

We are transforming the food system one garden at a time. In the last 6 years, our team of formerly incarcerated landscapers has built over 400 edible gardens throughout the East Bay, empowering hundreds of people to grow their own food. Now, we're cultivating urban farms and training centers that will dramatically increase the scope and scale of this work.

By building a local, sustainable food system, we can create thousands of green jobs. We provide living wages ($17.50/hr starting wage) and comprehensive health insurance to all our employees because our communities have been starved for good jobs for far too long.

Pop Up City

Location: International

Website: popupcity.net

The Pop-Up City is a blog that explores the latest designs, trends and ideas that shape the city of the future. We strongly focus on new concepts, strategies and methods for a dynamic and flexible interpretation of contemporary urban life.

The Pop-Up City is curated by the creative directors of Golfstromen, along with an international team of reporters.

Today's world cities deal with many problems related to rapidly increasing international societal, cultural, technological and economic transformation processes.

More variableness in economic, political and cultural patterns leads to new expectations and renewals of dynamic capacities of the city. Our aim is to search for creative solutions regarding flexible urbanism and architecture. We are located in downtown Amsterdam. Feel free to contact us for all your invitations, proposals, questions and tips.

Positively Paseo

Location: Oklahoma City, OK

Website: positivelypaseo.org

Positively Paseo is a 501(c)3 non-profit community housing development organization, or CHDO, working to revitalize the Paseo Historic District and Classen Ten Penn neighborhoods in Oklahoma City, Oklahoma. Our mission is to increase homeownership by providing families and individuals with low-to-moderate income levels the opportunity to purchase a rehabilitated, restored, or newly constructed home that is affordable and of good quality.

Like other inner-city Oklahoma City neighborhoods, Paseo and Classen Ten Penn suffered in the 70′s and 80′s when development began in the suburbs and drew families away from the center of the city.

In the mid 80's residents of Paseo and surrounding historic neighborhoods joined forces with area church officials, non-profit community associations, local bankers, and commercial property owners to set in place a plan to revitalize the Paseo neighborhood. Backed by an endorsement from a study by the Urban Land Institute in Washington D.C., Positively Paseo was formed to lead the way in housing rehabilitation.

Project for Public Spaces

Location: Nationwide

Website: pps.org

Project for Public Spaces (PPS) is a nonprofit planning, design and educational organization dedicated to helping people create and sustain public spaces that build stronger communities. Our pioneering "Placemaking" approach helps citizens transform their public spaces into vital places that highlight local assets, spur rejuvenation and serve common needs.

PPS was founded in 1975 to expand on the work of William (Holly) Whyte, the author of *The Social Life of Small Urban Spaces*. Since then, we have completed projects in over 2500 communities in 40 countries and all 50 US states. Partnering with public and private organizations, federal, state and municipal agencies, business improvement districts, neighborhood associations and other civic groups, we improve communities by fostering successful public spaces.

PPS also trains more than 10,000 people every year and reaches countless more through our websites and publications. PPS has become an internationally recognized center for resources, tools and inspiration about Placemaking.

PropertyPanel.LA

Location: Los Angeles, CA

Website: propertypanel.la

The City of Los Angeles, on behalf of its residents and taxpayers, owns a vast portfolio of real estate, encompassing nearly 9,000 distinct parcels located within the County of Los Angeles. These include parks, libraries, municipal facilities, parking lots, as well as commercial, industrial, retail, office and residential buildings and vacant land. Some are small, some are very large. L.A.'s real estate holdings also include land at and around our airports, the Port of L.A. and properties owned by our nation's largest municipally owned utility, the Dept. of Water & Power.

Properties owned by the city serve many community needs and benefits. There are, however, many properties that are underutilized, and which could better serve the public - be it as public space, revenue-producing income property, low-income housing and much more.

PropertyPanel.LA is intended as an informational tool, as a resource and as a call to action for the city to undertake a more organized, professional and strategic approach to our valuable shared public assets.

Philadelphia Citizens Planning Institute

Location: Philadelphia, PA

Website: citizenplanninginstitute.org

The focus of the Institute is to educate citizens about the role good planning and implementation play in helping to create communities of lasting value. Through education, we are building a constituency for good planning. Thanks to a generous grant from the William Penn Foundation, a pilot course was developed and delivered in 2010.

The series of three evening "Citizen Planner" classes provided '101' level introduction on planning issues and principles, land use and zoning, and the development process. The Mayor commended the 'learners' for their enthusiasm and commitment to Philadelphia and encouraged them to influence others with their passion for positive change through planning.

The Pilot Core Course has been improved and three "Electives" have been added to provide an overview of topics the pilot participants identified as useful: commercial development, transit-oriented development and healthy communities. Learners who successfully complete the classes comprising the core course and two of the three electives, will earn a Certificate of Completion as a "Citizen Planner" of Philadelphia.

placeful.

Location: Harlem, New York, NY

Website: placeful.org

placeful. is a non-profit 501(c)3 charitable organization with a mission to foster investment in community space through socially responsible partnerships in finance, agriculture, education and the arts. We believe that creative placemaking is key to our process and requires a combination of community empowerment, socially responsible real estate procedures and public-private finance for long term community benefit.

Our activities include community development, real estate development, and providing consulting services to projects that are committed to community infrastructure through financial, nutritional, educational and/or cultural programs and services. A core principle of our work is promoting values of "sustainability" within the practices and partnerships of community development.

Generally speaking, we believe "sustainable" practices use *triple bottom line* standards when assessing development: accounting for social, environmental and financial outcomes in any measure of success.

Prince's Foundation for Building Community

Location: Great Britain

Website: princes-foundation.org

The Prince's Foundation for Building Community (PFBC) evolved from The Institute of Architecture, established by HRH The Prince of Wales.

PFCB believes that sustainably planned, built and maintained communities improve the quality of life of everyone who is part of them. They help us live better at a local level, and start dealing with the broader global challenges of urbanisation and climate change.

By 2050, the world's urban population will almost double to nearly 6.5 billion people. PFCB operates across the globe, building the capacity of the planners, architects, engineers, and communities that will be tasked with supporting a rapidly urbanising world. Our work puts people at the heart of creating resilient places – through community engagement and working with people who know their area best. Through educating future generations of practitioners, pioneering practises, and building places, we endeavour to create sustainable, vibrant communities that leave a legacy for future generations.

Public Advocates

Location: California

Website: publicadvocates.org

Public Advocates Inc. is a nonprofit law firm and advocacy organization that challenges the systemic causes of poverty and racial discrimination by strengthening community voices in public policy and achieving tangible legal victories advancing education, housing and transit equity.

We spur change through collaboration with grassroots groups representing low-income communities, people of color and immigrants, combined with strategic policy reform, media advocacy and litigation, "making rights real" across California since 1971.

As a result of that engagement, all Californians have the building blocks to thrive and to create vibrant communities – excellent public schools, affordable housing, reliable public transportation, quality health care, good job opportunities, and economic security. We believe that by engaging in strategic partnerships, policy and media advocacy and litigation, we will increase the capacity of grassroots organizations to shape public policy and discourse, and that we can also positively influence public opinion, the media, policy makers and courts to hold business and government accountable.

Public Architecture

Location: San Francisco, CA

Website: publicarchitecture.org

Public Architecture is a new model for architectural practice. Supported by the generosity of foundation, corporate, and individuals grants and donations, Public Architecture works outside the economic constraints of conventional architectural practice, providing a venue where architects can work for the public good.

Rather than waiting for commissions that represent well understood needs and desires, we take a leadership role, identifying significant problems of wide relevance that require innovative research and design. We seek needs and desires that are palpable but poorly defined, in circumstances where both client and financing must be imagined in new ways.

We don't just do our own projects; we encourage architecture firms nationwide to formalize their commitment to the public good. While many architects give of their expertise from time to time, the profession as a whole has not structured its pro bono endeavors as clearly as has, say, the legal profession. "The 1%" program, through which firms pledge one percent of their billable hours to pro bono service, aims to institutionalize and celebrate pro bono practice in architecture.

Public Interest Design Institute

Location: Nationwide

Website: publicinterestdesign.com

There is a growing sector in the design professions known as Public Interest Design, as documented in MoMA's "Small Scale, Big Change " exhibit and publications like *Design Like You Give Damn*. The projects in this sector are unlike traditional practice in critical ways and are an area of great potential for the future of the design professions.

Public Interest Design Institutes (PIDI) provide training and in-depth study focused on how design professionals address critical issues faced by the communities we serve through collaborative processes and fee-based projects. Training in public interest design is a way of enhancing an existing practice by enhancing the skills needed to proactively engage in community-based design.

The PIDI curriculum is grounded in the Social Economic Environmental Design (SEED) mission, principles, and methodology. SEED goes beyond green design with a "triple bottom line" approach that tracks and documents social, economic, and environmental impact.

Puget Sound Sage

Location: Puget Sound Area, WA

Website: pugetsoundsage.org

Puget Sound Sage is an organization led by women of color that is accountable to and serves the interests of low-income people, communities of color, immigrants and refugees in the Puget Sound region of Washington State. In particular, we focus on Seattle, South King County and North Pierce County. We advocate for policy change at the local and regional level, where we believe community voices can have the most impact.

We have been a leading voice in the Puget Sound region over the last decade to ensure that all people thrive as our region grows and prospers. What makes Puget Sound Sage unique is that we work at the intersection of three elements critical to creating an equitable region: good jobs, a clean, healthy environment, and equitable development. By connecting the dots between these issues, we are more effective at systems change, innovation and engagement of communities.

We bring our expertise in strategic research, policy analysis, community organizing and coalition building to win local and regional campaigns that advance economic, racial and environmental justice.

Rails to Trails

Location: Nationwide

Website: railstotrails.org

Rails-to-Trails Conservancy (RTC) serves as the national voice for more than 160,000 members and supporters, 31,000 miles of rail-trails and multi-use trails, and more than 8,000 miles of potential trails waiting to be built, with a goal of creating more walkable, bikeable communities in America. Our national office is located in Washington, D.C., with regional offices in California, Florida, Ohio and Pennsylvania.

Since 1986, RTC has worked from coast to coast, supporting the development of thousands of miles of rail-trails for millions to explore and enjoy. We've helped craft rural trails that spool out over a hundred miles of open prairie, snake through mountain passes, span canyons and hug riverbanks, offering views of the countryside often unknown to the highway traveler. We've been a part of the connections between towns and suburbs, linking communities along vibrant corridors in much the same way as the railroads did in their heyday.

RTC's mission, and its value, is magnified in urban areas, where one mile of trail can completely redefine the livability of a community.

Rebuild Foundation

Location: Nationwide

Website: rebuiild-foundation.org

Rebuild Foundation helps neighborhoods thrive through culture-driven redevelopment by activating abandoned spaces with arts and cultural programming. We transform under-resourced communities by leveraging economic and cultural resources.

Rebuild hosted the 2012 Bruner Loeb Forum "The Art of Placemaking" conference and will break ground on the Dorchester Artist Housing Collaborative with the Chicago Housing Authority, transforming an empty housing project into a 36-unit complex with mixed income housing and a community arts center for programming, performance, and arts exhibitions.

Rebuild Foundation is a not-for-profit creative engine focused on cultural-driven redevelopment and affordable space initiatives in under-resourced communities, currently manages projects in Chicago, St. Louis and Omaha. Our programs enlist teams of artists, architects, developers, educators, community activists, and residents who work together to integrate the arts, apprenticeship trade training and creative entrepreneurship into a community-driven process of neighborhood transformation.

Reconnecting America

Location: Nationwide

Website: reconnectingamerica.org

Reconnecting America is a national nonprofit that advises civic and community leaders on how to overcome community development challenges to create better communities for all. Reconnecting America develops research and innovative public policy, while also building on-the-ground partnerships and convening players needed to accelerate decision-making.

The community where we live holds a special place in our hearts. Some of us still live in the same neighborhood where our family has had roots for generations. Some of us choose a community with an eye toward a new beginning. Where we live matters.

At Reconnecting America, we help transform promising ideas into thriving communities, where transportation choices make it easy to get from place to place, where businesses flourish, and where people from all walks of life can afford to live, work and visit.

Regional Plan Association

Location: CT, NY & NJ

Website: rpa.org

For 90 years, Regional Plan Association (RPA) has been an indispensable source of ideas and plans to policy makers and opinion shapers across the tri-state area. RPA's in-depth studies, relentless advocacy and staying power ensure that critical transportation, urban development, housing and open space projects move forward across business downturns and election cycles. And RPA's America 2050 program is advancing national efforts to strengthen our aging infrastructure and protect vital natural resources.

RPA has been helping guide the region's development of climate change and resiliency strategies, calling for a new approach to the way we manage storms in the tri-state region.

RPA has published influential research on why large infrastructure projects take so long to complete in the U.S. and how the work could be accelerated.

RPA has convened more than 125 national experts on large landscape conservation to discuss how to ensure that wildlife habitat, water supplies and working farms and forests throughout the U.S. Northeast are protected for future generations.

Reviving California

Location: Silicon Valley, CA

Website:
asoft484.securesites.net/secure/alfsiliconvalley/index.php?
src=gendocs&ref=reviving_ca_new_home

Reviving California is a project of the Common Good Collaborative, powered by American Leadership Forum (ALF) – Silicon Valley.

With initial funding from the John S. and James L. Knight Foundation, Reviving California (led by a steering committee of Senior Fellows) has played a significant role in reforming the state's fiscal and governance policies. By harnessing the power of networked leadership, Reviving California has directly influenced reform legislation and initiatives, including Open primaries and the recently completed redistricting process.

As part of this process, ALF has been helping Californians replace political rhetoric with authentic conversations, moving beyond the blame game, and creating the conditions for individuals, networks and communities to engage in democracy in an increasingly complex and diverse state.

Right to the City

Location: International

Website: righttothecity.org

Through shared principles and a common frame and theory of change, Right to the City (RTTC) is building a national movement for racial justice, urban justice, human rights, and democracy. RTTC seeks to create regional and national impacts in the fields of housing, human rights, urban land, community development, civic engagement, criminal justice, environmental justice, and more.

RTTC was born out of desire and need by organizers and allies around the country to have a stronger movement for urban justice. But it was also born out of the power of an idea of a new kind of urban politics that asserts that everyone, particularly the disenfranchised, not only has a right to the city, but as inhabitants, have a right to shape it, design it, and operationalize an urban human rights agenda.

In the realm of ideas, a key resource and touchstone is "Le droite à la ville" (Right to the City) a book published in 1968 by French intellectual and philosopher Henri Lefebvre. In the sphere of human rights, this powerful idea was adopted by the World Urban Forum and elaborated into the World Charter of the Right to the City in 2004.

River LA

Location: Los Angeles, CA

Website: riverla.com

The River LA will change the course of Los Angeles. Our objective is to create healthy, vibrant communities with greater open space, enhanced green infrastructure, and better recreational facilities.

We are a non-profit venture charged with catalyzing responsible real estate and related economic development along the LA River. Our mission is to transform the LA River to improve people's lives by carrying out sustainable land use projects, advocacy for river friendly policy, and programs for community benefit.

We are working to create a continuous 51-mile greenway corridor that will run along a restored LA River. Think of it as a linear Central Park—a grand public space that will redefine how we move through Los Angeles. The LA River can connect people throughout Los Angeles, restore natural habitat in some of the most park-poor communities in the country, and leave an open space legacy for generations to come. We can enhance the quality of life in a city hungry for green space and strengthen communities by restoring the LA River.

Sacramento Mobile Food

Location: Sacramento, CA

Website: www.sactomofo.com

Sacramento Mobile Food (SactoMoFo if you wanna get familiar) wants a level playing field for mobile kitchens. We believe these entrepreneurs deserve the same opportunities for success that other businesspeople enjoy, and to further awareness and build support we produce street food-centric events throughout the greater Sacramento region, to showcase their product, and their positive impact in our community.

Their tasty food is only the beginning. These small business owners buy local produce, meat and bread products, pay local sales taxes, add affordability and diversity to the local food scene, hire local workers, and offer aspiring restaurant owners an entry point into the possibility of the American Dream.

Some of the local food trucks are already well on their way there, and have opened local restaurants, created even more Sacramento jobs and have generated thousands of dollars in sales taxes. Additionally, food truck owners are heavily vested in their local communities and generously give back.

San Franciscans for Planning and Urban Research

Location: San Francisco, CA

Website: spur.org

Through research, education and advocacy, San Franciscans for Planning and Urban Research (SPUR) promotes good planning and good government in the San Francisco Bay Area. SPUR's history dates back to 1910, when a group of young city leaders came together to improve the quality of housing after the 1906 earthquake and fire. That group, the San Francisco Housing Association, authored a hard-hitting report which led to the State Tenement House Act of 1911.

In the 1950s, San Francisco Planning and Housing Association (SFPHA) pushed for the revitalization of San Francisco as the Bay Area's central city, in an effort to curb suburban sprawl and channel growth back into the urban core. In 1959, the SFPHA was reorganized into the San Francisco Planning and Urban Renewal Association—and later, the San Francisco Planning and Urban Research Association—to be the citizens' voice for good planning.

Over the next five decades, SPUR built support for land use, transportation and investment strategies to support center-oriented growth and urban economic vitality.

San Francisco Bicycle Coalition

Location: San Francisco, CA

Website: sfbike.org

The San Francisco Bicycle Coalition (SFBC) is one of the oldest bicycle advocacy organizations in the country. Founded in 1971 by a group of activists representing a coalition of environmental and neighborhood groups, the SFBC started the convention of calling an advocacy group a "coalition" while riding groups were known as clubs.For over 40 years, the SFBC has been transforming San Francisco's streets and neighborhoods into more livable and safe places by promoting the bicycle for everyday transportation.

Through our day-to-day advocacy, education, and working partnerships with government and community agencies, we are helping create safer streets and more livable communities for all San Franciscans.

Our active 12,000 members represent San Franciscans of all ages, from all neighborhoods, who are working towards more safe, efficient, and fun ways to move around our city. The SFBC is the largest city-based bicycle advocacy group in the nation and one of the largest membership-based groups in San Francisco. Our members donated over 16,000 volunteer hours in 2011.

San Francisco Beautiful

Location: San Francisco, CA

Website: sfbeautiful.org

San Francisco is beautiful because we make it that way. When our plazas need help, we refresh them. Our vision is to keep San Francisco beautiful.

Our mission is to create, enhance, and maintain the unique beauty and livability of San Francisco.

For more than 60 years, San Francisco Beautiful — a group of citizens, neighbors, friends, and philanthropists — has been integral in making San Francisco the extraordinary place it is today.

We work to keep San Francisco beautiful through civic engagement, partnering with communities to build better neighborhoods, and celebrating urban innovation.

If you love San Francisco, we love you. Join now to keep San Francisco beautiful.

San Francisco Housing Action Coalition

Location: San Francisco, CA

Website: sfhac.org

The San Francisco Housing Action Coalition (SFHAC) is a small, lean operation with a staff of two, an executive director and a project manager. From the start, our work has largely been done by the amazing community of volunteers and activists from our member organizations in three long-running committees as dictated in our bylaws.

The Endorsement Committee reviews and discusses proposed projects to see how they match up with our endorsement guidelines. If we endorse a project, the SFHAC becomes one of the few groups to advocate for it at public hearings and in the entitlement process. This is not a small service in a city with such strong NIMBY views.

The Regulatory Committee addresses housing and land use policy and legislation. In a city like ours, there are always policy proposals. Where they advance SFHAC's mission we support them and push to get them enacted. Where they are harmful to our mission, we work to modify them to cause the least harm possible to our mission.

San Francisco Tenants Union

Location: San Francisco, CA

Website: www.sftu.org

Since 1971, the San Francisco Tenants Union (SFTU) has been fighting for the rights of tenants and for the preservation of affordable housing in San Francisco. From the struggle for rent control in the 1970's to 1998's Proposition G (to end the abuses of owner or relative move-in evictions), the Tenants Union has been the city's leading advocate for tenants. The SFTU is 100% membership supported and this enables our advocacy to be uncompromising and immune to pressures from government or other funders.

For both members and non-members, the SFTU operates a drop in counseling clinic at 558 Capp Street (in the Mission District - cross street is 21st Street. Counseling hours are available by appointment.

Counseling is free for SFTU members. Non-members are asked to donate ($20 for people of moderate incomes or above, $10 for people with low incomes) per visit (no one is turned away for lack of funds, however).

Santa Monica Coalition for a Liveable City

Location: Santa Monica, CA

Website: smclc.net

Santa Monica Coalition for a Livable City (SMCLC) is a nonprofit, all volunteer group of Santa Monica residents concerned about unsustainable commercial development in our city, the effects it has on traffic and our quality of life, and the influence developer money has on our local elections.

Through education, advocacy, and organizing, SMCLC works to ensure that residents have meaningful input into the development decisions that affect their lives.

Keeping Santa Monica livable, requiring new growth to be on a scale that is both sane and sustainable, and ensuring transparency in local government are all key goals of SMCLC. SMCLC is a California 501(c)4 organization.

Save Open Space and Agricultural Resources

Location: Ventura County, California

Website: soarvc.org

Save Open Space and Agricultural Resources (SOAR) is a series of voter initiatives that require a vote of the people before agricultural land or open space areas can be rezoned for development. The first SOAR initiative was approved by the voters in the City of Ventura in 1995. Since 1995, nine SOAR initiatives have been enacted protecting open space and agricultural land around all of the major cities in Ventura County as well as in the county's unincorporated areas.

The County SOAR initiative blocks the Ventura County Board of Supervisors from rezoning unincorporated open space, agricultural or rural land for development without a vote of the people. Eight city SOAR initiatives require city councils to obtain the approval of their citizens before allowing urban development beyond a City Urban Restriction Boundary (CURB), or, in the case of the City of Ventura, before rezoning agricultural land within the city's sphere of influence.

SOAR is a non-profit grassroots group of citizens in Ventura County, California.

Save The Bay

Location: San Francisco Bay Area, CA

Website: savesfbay.org

Save The Bay is the largest regional organization working to protect, restore and celebrate San Francisco Bay. As its leading champion since 1961, Save The Bay protects the San Francisco Bay from pollution and inappropriate shoreline development, making it cleaner and healthier for people and wildlife.

We restore habitat and secure strong policies to re-establish 100,000 acres of wetlands that are essential for a healthy bay.

We engage more than 40,000 supporters, advocates and volunteers to protect the bay, and inspire the next generation of environmental leaders by educating thousands of students annually.

Shape My City

Location: Toronto, Ontario

Website: shapemycity.org

Shape My City is your invitation to join Toronto's active network for people who are passionate about making this city a place where everyone can engage, where everyone can thrive.

Shape My City is your local matchmaker to connect with people, groups and communities across Toronto that will fuel your city-shaping and community-building passions.

Shape My City is your "action central to get creative. Embrace your inner activist! Access tons of let's-make-it-happen tools and resources. Help build extraordinary events and movements – like YIMBY (Yes in my backyard) and more!

Shape My City is your platform connect, create and share. Let's shape something great!

Shape My City is your story.

Shelterforce

Location: International

Website: shelterforce.org

Shelterforce is the nation's oldest continuously published housing and community development magazine. For more than three decades, Shelterforce has been a primary forum for organizers, activists, and advocates in the affordable housing and neighborhood revitalization movements.

National Housing Institute (NHI) is an independent nonprofit organization that examines the issues causing the crisis in housing and community in America. These issues include poverty and racism, disinvestment and lack of employment, safety, education, and breakdown of the social fabric. NHI examines how these and other factors affect people as they try to build safe, viable neighborhoods. NHI searches for what does and does not work in community-building.

NHI is dedicated to providing the tools (information, analysis, resources) for advocates, activists, and community members to organize their communities, rebuild their neighborhoods, and create decent housing and living wage jobs for the families who live there.

Sierra Business Council

Location: California

Website: sbcouncil.org

Sierra Business Council (SBC) is a member-based organization of over 700 individuals and businesses who are committed to pioneering innovative solutions in the Sierra Nevada.

SBC has been walking the talk since 1994. We are the Sierra Nevada's sustainability organization and continue to demonstrate that vibrant communities, fair and prosperous economies, and healthy thriving ecosystems are not competing interests. When all three thrive, everyone wins. Our primary mission is to pioneer innovative approaches and solutions that foster community vitality, environmental quality, economic prosperity, and social fairness in the Sierra Nevada.

In the Sierra Nevada, change and challenge create opportunities. Through innovation, integrity, and respect, the SBC fosters and harnesses these opportunities by implementing and modeling proactive adaptation to a shifting environment, economy, and population. We have partnered with many individuals and organizations throughout the Sierra to create a plethora of publications.

Sightline Institute

Location: Northwest U.S.

Website: sightline.org

Sightline Institute's (SI) mission is to make the Northwest a global model of sustainability— strong communities, a green economy, and a healthy environment. Our purpose as an organization is to provide Cascadia's community problem solvers with practical vision and innovative thinking, inspiring and empowering them to bring about a healthy, lasting prosperity. We like to think of ourselves as sowers of seeds—planting ideas and stewarding their growth so sustainable solutions can flourish.

Founded in 1993, SI is committed to making the Northwest a global model of sustainability, with strong communities, a green economy, and a healthy environment. We work to promote smart policy ideas and monitor the region's progress towards sustainability.

SI believes that true sustainability exists at the intersection of environmental health and social justice. Our core values: community, fairness, opportunity, and responsibility center on that principle, and our work over the last ten years to understand and prioritize diversity, equity, and inclusion have found a firm foundation there.

Silicon Valley Rising

Location: Silicon Valley, CA

Website: siliconvalleyrising.org

Silicon Valley Rising (SVR) is a coordinated campaign driven by an unprecedented coalition of labor, faith leaders, community-based organizations and workers.

SVR aspires to a new vision for Silicon Valley where all workers, their families and communities are valued. We have high expectations for this Valley and for our communities:

We want to be a part of creating a new economic model that rebuilds the middle class.

We want to raise wages and standards for all workers so they can live and thrive here.

And we want to build housing that is affordable and accessible so that our families don't have to live in garages, in their cars, or near a creekbed.

SVR's campaign is about bringing everyone in this Valley together to solve the biggest challenges of our time.

Slum Dwellers International

Location: International

Website: sdinet.org

Slum Dwellers International (SDI) is a network of community based organizations of the urban poor in 33 countries in Africa, Asia, and Latin America.

In each country where SDI has a presence, affiliate organizations come together at the community, city, and national level rooted in specific methodologies. SDI's mission is to link urban poor communities from cities that have developed successful mobilisation, advocacy, and problem solving strategies. Since SDI is focused on the localized needs of slum dwellers, it has developed the traction to advance the common agenda of creating "pro-poor" cities that address the pervasive exclusion of the poor from the economies and political structures of 21st century cities.

Further, SDI uses its global reach to build a platform for slum dwellers to engage directly with governments and international organizations to try new strategies, change policies, and build understanding about the challenges of urban development.

Social Economic Environmental Design Network

Location: Nationwide

Websie: seed-network.org

The Social Economic Environmental Design (SEED) Network connects similarly-minded members of the general public with designers from the fields of Architecture, Communication Design, Industrial Design, Landscape Architecture, Urban Design, and Urban Planning, who have an interest in community-based design practice. The network is comprised of SEED members-individuals, groups, or organizations that support the SEED mission and principles through their own practices.

SEED is a principle-based network of individuals and organizations dedicated to building and supporting a culture of civic responsibility and engagement in the built environment and the public realm. By sharing best practices and ideas, these parties create a community of knowledge for professionals and the public based on a set of shared principles.

The SEED Network members promote and celebrate the idea that design matters and all people can shape their world for the better through design. The network is part of a global movement that believes design can support a community from the ground up.

Society for Commercial Archeology

Location: Nationwide

Website: sca-roadside.org

Drew University defines Commercial Archeology as: "The study of structures and artifacts created in connection with popular commercial activity, such as diners, motels, gasoline stations, and signs." Kris Hirst at About.com offers this definition: "Commercial archaeology focuses on the material culture aspects of commerce and transportation; studies the effects of market economy and the use of space, and the development of roadside businesses."

The term roadside architecture applies to buildings and other structures directly and indirectly associated with roads. Obvious examples include restaurants, motels and gas stations. Other examples include signs, vernacular buildings, shopping and retail centers, programmatic (or mimetic) structures as well as theme and amusement parks.

The Society for Commercial Archeology was organized by a group of scholars and experts who had an interest in commercial archeology. The group met in Vermont and in 1979, they formally organized. At present, the operations of the SCA are managed throughout the country by the members of the board of directors. SCA maintains an archive of its own materials in Austin, Texas.

Society for the Promotion of Area Resource Centers

Location: India

Website: sparcindia.org

The Society for the Promotion of Area Resource Centres (SPARC) is one of the largest Indian NGOs working on these issues. SPARC supports two people's movements, the National Slum Dwellers Federation and Mahila Milan, in organizing the urban poor to come together, articulate their concerns and collectively produce solutions to the problems they face.

SPARC was formed in 1984 and began working with the most vulnerable and invisible of Mumbai's urban poor – the pavement dwellers. SPARC's philosophy is that if we can develop solutions that work for the poorest and most marginalised in the city, then these solutions can be scaled up to work for other groups of the urban poor across the country and internationally.

The ultimate aim of the Alliance is to produce urban and development practices and policies that are inclusive of the poor. Our mission is to build the capacity of organized communities of the urban poor, especially women, in informal settlements to stop forced evictions and develop the skills and confidence to negotiate with the government and other resource providers.

226

SolidarityNYC

Location: New York, NY

Website: solidaritynyc.org

SolidarityNYC connects, supports, and promotes New York City's solidarity economy.

The solidarity economy meets human needs through economic activities–like the production and exchange of goods and services–that reinforce values of justice, ecological sustainability, cooperation, and democracy. From credit unions to worker cooperatives, community supported agriculture to time banks, community land trusts to participatory budgeting, it's an economy actually worth occupying.

Our vision is a vibrant and growing movement that provides greater economic security, improved physical and emotional health, and increased democracy for our communities and ecosystems.

We hope to make the strong solidarity economy practices that already exist in New York City more visible and bring the various sectors of the solidarity economy into conversation with each other for collaboration and mutual benefit.

Son of a Saint

Location: New Orleans, LA

Website: sonofasaint.org

Each year we select ten boys to join the existing kids in our program. The boys must be fatherless due to their father's incarceration or death. Boys enter our program between the ages of 10 and 13 years old and remain members of the group until they receive their college acceptance letter.

One of the biggest challenges some of our kids face relate to self-confidence, anger, and feeling of abandonment. We partner with Loving Hearts Social Services of New Orleans and various mental health agencies to provide evaluations and ongoing counseling for our boys.

Daylong sessions are held once a month and are designed to aid in the academic, personal, and overall development of our kids. Sessions are held at local colleges in order to expose the kids to that environment and help them realize that higher education is an attainable goal and worthy of aspiration. Topics of mentorship sessions have included: etiquette, time management, decision making skills, critical thinking, anger management, moral reasoning, life skills training, work ethic, leadership, civic responsibility, teamwork and integrity.

Sonoran Institute

Location: Western United States

Website: sonoraninstitute.org

The Sonoran Institute inspires and enables community decisions and public policies that respect the land and people of western North America.

The Sonoran Institute contributes to a vision of a West with: healthy landscapes including native plants and wildlife, diverse habitat, open spaces, clean air and water, from northern Mexico to western Canada, where people embrace conservation to protect quality of life today and in the future and resilient economies that support prosperous communities, diverse opportunities for residents, productive working landscapes, and stewardship of the natural world.

The nonprofit Sonoran Institute, founded in 1990, works across the rapidly changing West to conserve and restore natural and cultural assets and to promote better management of growth and change. The Institute's community-based approach emphasizes collaboration, civil dialogue, sound information, local knowledge, practical solutions and big-picture thinking.

Southeast Food Access

Location: San Francisco, CA

Website: southeastfoodaccess.org

Southeast Food Access (SEFA) is a collaborative of residents, community based organizations, city agencies, and others working on food access and food systems. SEFA's goal is to leverage similar efforts and encourage partnerships and collaboration in order to achieve a vibrant and robust food system for all in Bayview Hunters Point (BVHP). As such, SEFA has identified three pillars that are integral to a robust food system and which guide our work: food access, awareness/education, and urban agriculture.

SEFA has been particularly focused on bringing healthier food retail and grocery options to the neighborhood. In 2007, SEFA members conducted and released a resident food preferences survey which was instrumental for efforts by the Mayor's Office of Economic and Workforce Development to recruit a new food retailer, Fresh and Easy to the neighborhood. We continue to work with BVHP food retailers to increase their offerings of fresh, affordable and healthy foods.

SEFA and the Food Guardians are key partners in the Bayview HEAL Zone initiative, funded by Kaiser Permanente, to promote healthy eating and active living.

Sprockets St. Paul

Location: St. Paul, MN

Website: sprocketsaintpaul.org

Sprockets is a partnership between the Center for Democracy and Citizenship and the City of Saint Paul through the Second Shift Initiative with the Saint Paul Public School District, Saint Paul Federation of Teachers union, and many community-based organizations and individuals.

Working together, we aim to ensure that young people in Saint Paul grow up in a culture of learning that spans the many learning environments that impact their academic achievement, skill development, and personal growth so that they successfully meet the demands and expectations for the 21st century.

The Center for Democracy and Citizenship uses the lens of public work, in which people from diverse backgrounds work across differences to solve public problems, create public goods, and build thriving, inclusive communities. A public work approach to education–building on rich traditions of formal and informal learning that emphasize young people's capacities for productive contribution and focuses on how every young person can be successful as an individual and a citizen.

Square One Villages

Location: Eugene, OR

Website: squareonevillages.org

Square One Village is a pilot project that will provide transitional micro-housing for 30-40 homeless individuals and couples at a time. Design and organization of the village will be based upon best practices derived from a comprehensive study of long standing "tent cities" in the United States, lessons learned from local encampments, and a creative understanding of permaculture principles.

The transitional micro-housing will be compact (60-100 square feet) and transportable (less than 8 feet wide).

The idea is to combine a sense of ownership over a small, private space with an abundance of shared, common spaces that include cooking facilities, gathering areas, restrooms, and micro-business opportunities. The village will be built through a collaboration between village residents, community volunteers, and skilled builders. The Village will be self-managed with oversight provided by a 501(c)3 Board of Directors. Basic rules will be upheld through a community agreement that prohibits stealing, violence, and drug or alcohol use.

St. Bernard Project

Location: New Orleans, LA

Website: sbpusa.org

The St. Bernard Project (SBP) was launched to help the community achieve its recovery goals. With the tremendous support of donors, volunteers and corporate partners, SBP has grown from a three-person volunteer team into a nationally recognized leader in disaster resilience and recovery.

The key to SBP's programmatic success is our model, an all under one-roof and vertically integrated approach that provides clients with one point of contact, causes efficiencies and accountability between traditionally siloed components and eliminates the need for (and cost of) subcontractors through in-house skilled labor crews.

SBP's model is deeply subsidized by AmeriCorps members from all over the country who serve as client case managers, volunteer coordinators, and construction site supervisors, overseeing the labor of more than 10,000 volunteers, per location, each year SBP saves time and money by exercising direct control over skilled labor and scheduling, which also allows us to create well paying jobs for veterans and other under and unemployed residents.

Steel Yard

Location: Providence, RI

Website: thesteelyard.org

The Steel Yard offers arts and technical training programs designed to increase opportunities for cultural and artistic expression, career-oriented training, and small business incubation.

Our work is made possible through a combination of program-related earned income, private and government grants, corporate giving and individual philanthropy.

We are located at the historic Providence Steel and Iron site, along the Woonasquatucket River in the heart of Providence's industrial Valley neighborhood.

Our 10,000 square foot industrial shop includes: welding, blacksmithing, jewelry, ceramics, and foundry space, ceramics cooperative, jewelry cooperative, studio access opportunities, and outdoor multi-use work and exhibition space.

The Steel Yard programs cater to working artists, students, community members, tradespeople, arts educators and entrepreneurs.

streets.mn

Location: Minnesota

Website: streets.mn

streets.mn explores the pressing issues facing our cities, towns, neighborhood and the places in between. Our mission is to expand and enhance the conversation about transportation and land use through research and informed commentary.

streets.mn was formed because we think transportation and land use news and information in Minnesota can be done better. Content for streets.mn is produced by these fine folks. streets.mn is 100% member-supported and volunteer-driven. streets.mn is a non-profit organization, governed by our board.

streets.mn is authored by a diverse group of contributors. The views, opinions, and positions expressed by each author and those providing comments are theirs alone, and do not necessarily reflect the views, opinions or positions of the streets.mn Board or any other site contributor.

Strong Towns

Location: Nationwide

Website: strongtowns.org

The American approach to growth is causing economic stagnation and decline along with land use practices that force a dependency on public subsidies. The inefficiencies of the current approach have left American towns financially insolvent, unable to pay even the maintenance costs of their basic infrastructure. A new approach that accounts for the full cost of growth is needed to make our towns strong again.

The Strong Towns approach ultimately requires a reorientation of emphasis and a renewed understanding of what it takes to build a town or a neighborhood. The current approach to growth emphasizes investments in new infrastructure to serve or induce new development. This approach uses public dollars inefficiently, destructively subsidizes one type of development over another and leaves massive maintenance liabilities to future generations.

A Strong Town approach emphasizes obtaining a higher return on existing infrastructure investments. We can no longer simply disregard old investments in favor of new, but instead we need to focus on making better use of that which we are already committed to publicly maintain.

Sunlight Foundation

Location: Washington, DC

Website: sunlightfoundation.com

The Sunlight Foundation is a nonprofit, nonpartisan organization that uses the power of the Internet to catalyze greater government openness and transparency, and provides new tools and resources for media and citizens, alike. We are committed to improving access to government information by making it available online, indeed redefining "public" information as meaning "online," and by creating new tools and websites to enable individuals and communities to better access that information and put it to use.

We want to catalyze greater government transparency by engaging individual citizens and communities -- technologists, policy wonks, open government advocates and ordinary citizens -- demanding policies that will enable all of us to hold government accountable.

Sunlight develops and encourages new government policies to make it more open and transparent, facilitates searchable, sortable and machine readable databases, builds tools and websites to enable easy access to information and fosters distributed research projects as a community building tool.

Sustainable Northwest

Location: Oregon and Washington

Website: sustainablenorthwest.org

We envision a thriving Northwest with strong communities, vibrant economies, and healthy and productive landscapes. We are a non-profit organization based in Portland, Oregon that bridges multiple stakeholders to solve natural resource management issues in rural communities.

Founded in 1994, Sustainable Northwest is a pioneer in solving problems through collaboration and has grown into one of the most trusted organizations working at the intersection of the environment, economy, and community. Sustainable Northwest brings people, ideas, and innovation together so that nature, local economies, and rural communities can thrive. Our work results in restored ecosystems, living wage jobs, and better relationships among diverse groups of people.

We work with communities to innovate and solve critical natural resource challenges. Our unique approach is to listen, learn, build trust, and be invested in the long term success of the communities and region we serve.

Sustainable SITES Initiative

Location: International

Website: sustainablesites.org

The SITES program was developed through a collaborative, interdisciplinary effort of the American Society of Landscape Architects, The Lady Bird Johnson Wildflower Center at The University of Texas at Austin, and the United States Botanic Garden.

The U.S. Green Building Council (USGBC) has been a long-time supporter and stakeholder in the Sustainable SITES Initiative. USGBC has incorporated certain SITES credit content into iterations of the LEED green building rating system. Likewise, SITES has adapted LEED credits as part of its SITES v2 Rating System, when relevant and appropriate.

Green Business Certification Inc. (GBCI) provides project certification to the requirements of the SITES v2 Rating System. Over the years, the SITES program has received numerous awards.

Sustainia

Location: International

Website: sustainiaworld.com

Sustainia is a sustainability advisory group and digital studio working to accelerate action towards a greener and fairer future. Since 2009, we've been working with private and public organizations, helping them move sustainability into the core of their activities by developing cutting-edge strategies, building engaging digital solutions, and amplifying their messages with impact. We are founders of The Sustainian – the global market guide for leaders.

We are founders of Global Opportunity Explorer – with United Nations Global Compact (a voluntary initiative based on CEO commitments to implement universal sustainability principles and to take steps to support UN goals) and DNVGL (a global quality assurance and risk management company).

We believe reaching the UN Global Goals by 2030 requires a bold vision, great leadership and swift action, and we are ready to help you take the next step.Behind every risk there is always an opportunity. On February 1, we released the fourth Global Opportunity Report with DNVGL and the UNGC, which shows how we can turn some of the world's biggest risks into sustainable business opportunities.

Sustaining Ourselves Locally

Location: Oakland, CA

Website: oaklandsol.weebly.com

In the industrial concrete landscape of East Oakland, sandwiched between the roaring BART trains and the rumbling stream of traffic on International Boulevard, sits an unlikely earthen oasis where sun-kissed organic tomatoes ripen on vines, neat rows of two-story-high corn stalks and greens await harvest, and plump chickens pick at the ground, oblivious to the urban bustle surrounding them.

Founded in 2003, Saving Ourselves Locally (SOL) incorporated as a 501(c)3 nonprofit in 2018 that shares sustainable practices and promoting social justice through education and community building.

SOL is a collectively run volunteer organization of 6 members. We work on social justice and food justice by opening our doors to events, hosting urban gardening days, and sponsoring political education through a paid youth summer internship. Our 5,000 square foot organic garden houses eight rotating food plots, an herb spiral, greenhouse, chicken-coop, and natives section, and provides habitat for hummingbirds, a turtle, and countless other urban critters and insects.

synerG

Location: Greensboro, NC

Website: synerg.org

synerG, under the umbrella of Action Greensboro, is an active organization of young adults who lead initiatives with the mission to attract, engage and connect young professionals to Greensboro, North Carolina.

Through our projects, synerG promotes social and professional networking, leadership opportunities and serves as a clearinghouse for information for young adults in the 21-39 year-old age demographic. synerG values the creation of opportunities and atmospheres that promote connectedness, diversity/inclusiveness and accessibility.

In 2001, Action Greensboro commissioned the McKinsey Report on the state of economic growth in Greensboro. One strong finding was that Greensboro had been seeing a decline in numbers of 18-34 year olds in the past decade.

During the same time period, Raleigh and Charlotte had been able to attract young people from outside their county lines, increasing their absolute number of young residents and bucking the national trend toward an aging population. With this challenge, Action Greensboro created synerG.

Taylor Community Science Resource Center

Location: St. Louis, MO

Website:
slsc.org/ForEducators/TaylorCommunityCenter.aspx

The Taylor Center is a dynamic place, providing outreach and community programs for youngsters of all ages, adults, and educators. Through its myriad partnerships and collaborations throughout the community, the Science Center has seen a growing need for high quality math and science based programming.

The Taylor Center is a place where learning happens every day, where teachers connect with science and technology, and where youngsters are actively engaged. The Taylor Center meets one of the metropolitan area's most critical needs - one facility that provides high-quality information about science and technology for many different audiences, including educators, parents, teens and community-based organizations.

The facility houses several classrooms and multipurpose rooms that can be used for after-school programming, professional development for educators, community-wide and family programming and more.

TEDCity 2.0

Location: International

Website: tedcity2.org

Through events and the sharing of ideas, TEDCity2.0 carries forward the 2012 TED Prize and advances us toward The City 2.0. Moreover, it builds on multiple initiatives from the early years of the Prize, including a micro-grant awards program, TEDx gatherings around the world, and an array of other programming.

The City 2.0 website was a platform created to surface the myriad stories and collective actions being taken by citizens around the world. The City 2.0 has evolved from a platform for the best of what is already being discovered by urban advocates and grassroots movers and shakers, to TEDCity2.0, content that celebrates a complex picture of the future city–a place more playful, more safe, more beautiful, and more healthy for everyone.

The TED Prize is awarded annually to a leader with a fresh, bold vision for sparking global change. The TED Prize winner receives $1,000,000 — and the TED community's wide range of resources and expertise — to make their dream become a reality.

Terwilliger Center for Housing

Location: Nationwide

Website: uli.org/research/centers-initiatives/terwilliger-center-for-housing

The ULI Terwilliger Center for Housing engages in a multifaceted program of work that includes research, publications, convenings, awards, and technical assistance. Our mission is to facilitate creating and sustaining a full spectrum of housing opportunities—including affordable and workforce housing—in communities across the country.

Established in 2007 with a gift from longtime ULI member and former ULI chairman J. Ronald Terwilliger, the Center's initial mission was to expand workforce housing opportunities for families earning 60 to 120 percent of the area median income.

While the Center's primary focus remains on housing affordability, with a particular emphasis on workforce housing policies and projects, our mission has expanded in 2011 to include a broader range of housing issues. This expanded focus will help to integrate ULI's many housing efforts into a coherent program of work that furthers the development of mixed-income, mixed-use communities and a full spectrum of housing affordable to all.

Texas Organizing Project

Location: Texas

Website: organizetexas.org

Texas Organizing Project (TOP) organizes Black and Latino communities in Dallas, Harris and Bexar counties with the goal of transforming Texas into a state where working people of color have the power and representation they deserve. Texas is a big and diverse state, and considering the evolving social makeup and the widespread need for improvement in areas of health care, poverty and education, community organizing has never been more important in Texas than it is today.

TOP provides hard working Texans the opportunity to implement real change by organizing their own neighborhoods, investing their time and energy in causes relevant to their respective communities, and collectively taking ownership over TOP's agenda, strategy and direction.

With a seasoned and committed organizing staff, a diverse membership and leaders from all walks of life, TOP has already made a huge impact and is positioned to continue to grow.

TimeBanks

Location: Nationwide

Website: timebanks.org

Timebanking is a time-based currency. Give one hour of service to another, and receive one time credit. You can use the credits in turn to receive services — or you can donate them to others. Unlike money, where some work is valued highly, and other work is given little value, an hour of service is always one time credit regardless of the nature of the service performed.

It can be hard for us to wrap our heads around this One = One rule because we are so used to regular money which includes price, and where some kinds of work earn a lot while other kinds of work earn very little. It helps to remember that this rule is rooted in the idea that regardless of whether we value what we *do* in different ways, we share a fundamental equality as human beings.

The focus is often on exchanges by individual members as they give and receive services to each other, forming a different kind of local economy based on caring and kindness. TimeBanks include group and community projects.

Town Square Initiative

Location: International

Website: gensleron.com/cities

Our cities need to become better at what they do. They must provide comprehensive answers to help balance and foster our lifestyles on a global level. The time is now, and those of us who can have an obligation to contribute to and even to instigate dialogues on how to best achieve this.

Gensler is taking on this challenge by launching the Reimagining Cities campaign. Each year, our offices around the globe will explore one topic that defines modern cities and seek out, in the places Gensler calls home, ways to demonstrate innovative urban ideas.

TSI was the inaugural effort for Reimagining Cities. The primary focus of this yearlong volunteer effort was to reconsider the public open spaces in cities and to explore how we can improve our social capacity through an improved physical urban environment. Over the last 12 months more than half of Gensler's offices worldwide engaged in this initiative to improve the urban environment.

Transportation Alternatives

Location: New York, NY

Website: transalt.org

Transportation Alternatives (TA) is New York City's leading transportation advocacy organization, with a citywide network of 100,000 active supporters committed to reclaiming New York City's streets for people by ensuring that every New Yorker has safe space to walk and bike and access to public transportation. Every day, all over the city, we're working to make New York City's neighborhoods safer and restore a vibrant culture of street life.

TA is involved in every aspect of traveling around New York City. From bike routes and bus lanes to pedestrian crossings and play streets, we're fighting for safer, smarter transportation and a healthier city.

Since our founding in 1973 TA has helped New York City's bicycling population grow exponentially and worked to dramatically reduce the number of pedestrians killed each year by dangerous drivers. In the early 2000s, TA introduced New York's policymakers to the idea of bus-only lanes, laying the foundation for the swift new Select Bus Service in 2007.

Treepedia

Location: International

Website: senseable.mit.edu/treepedia

Which cities have the greenest streets? MIT's Senseable City Lab is pushing toward an answer to this question with a new project called Treepedia – a map website that catalogues the density of the tree canopy in 10 global cities, Treepedia uses information from Google Street View to create what it calls the Green View Index—a rating that quantifies how green a street view looks according to the number of trees it contains.

Rating a huge number of street corners for the relative greenery of their appearance, Treepedia also allows browsers to click on a series of dots that reveal street view images of the location in question. The result is one of the most detailed catalogs of urban greenery available.

While the site currently only maps around ten cities, it's a growing resource that could someday contain information about streets all over the world. The tool should allow residents to compare neighborhoods within their cities and cities to each other. Giving a visual, quantifiable testament to tree cover may make it easier to examine the issue in terms that are concrete and compelling.

Tree Pittsburgh

Location: Pittsburgh, PA

Website: treepittsburgh.org

Tree Pittsburgh is an environmental non-profit organization dedicated to enhancing the city's vitality by restoring and protecting the urban forest through tree maintenance, planting, education and advocacy.

Our vision is to be a leader in creating a healthy, attractive and safe urban forest by inspiring and engaging citizens to plant, maintain and protect trees. Trees provide substantial environmental, social and economic benefits that greatly enhance our quality of life.

There is so much to learn about trees - how to maintain them, protect them, to speak on their behalf. This website is designed to equip you with the knowledge necessary to assist Tree Pittsburgh in meeting our mission to protect and maintain our precious urban forest.

T.R.U.S.T. South LA

Location: Los Angeles, CA

Website: trustsouthla.org

T.R.U.S.T South LA is a community land trust was established in 2005 as a democratic and permanent steward of land, to challenge the role that speculators, absentee owners and corporations have played in deciding the neighborhoods' future. With grant and loan funds raised from public and private sources, the Land Trust acquires land to be held in perpetuity by the community-controlled land trust. The land will be leased for the development of affordable family housing and other community-serving uses.

Permanent control over the assets of the land trust is ensured by its legal structure as a membership organization, with regular members restricted to low-income people who live or work in the land trust area. Our principles guide how we engage our community, educate and develop our consciousness, skills, and experience individually and collectively.

We take responsibility to understand the context of the community, and our environment and together create a strategic plan, develop a new generation of leadership through sharing tools, knowledge and creating opportunities for youth.

United Nations Global Compact

Location: International

Website: unglobalcompact.org

In 2015, all 193 Member States of the United Nations adopted a plan for achieving a better future for all — laying out a path over the next 15 years to end extreme poverty, fight inequality and injustice, and protect our planet. At the heart of "Agenda 2030" are the 17 Sustainable Development Goals (SDGs) which clearly define the world we want — applying to all nations and leaving no one behind.

The new Global Goals result from a process that has been more inclusive than ever, with Governments involving business, civil society and citizens from the outset. We are all in agreement on where the world needs to go. Fulfilling these ambitions will take an unprecedented effort by all sectors in society — and business has to play a very important role in the process.

To make this happen, the UN Global Compact supports companies to: do business responsibly by aligning their strategies and operations with Ten Principles on human rights, labour, environment and anti-corruption; and take strategic actions to advance broader societal goals, such as the UN Sustainable Development Goals, with an emphasis on collaboration and innovation.

Urban Assembly

Location: New York, NY

Website: urbanassembly.org

The Urban Assembly was founded in 1990 to address a wide range of poverty issues. In the mid 90's we spearheaded a major planning effort to transform a 300-block area of the South Bronx. That effort identified the lack of high-quality local secondary schools as a major concern and recommended creating three model high schools, each tied to a major local institution.

We are reaching into the communities where kids need us most and giving thousands of students the education they deserve.

By every measure, our children are among the city's most underserved - 94% of our students are African-American and Latino. 69% of our students qualify for free and reduced lunch programs. 70% of 9th graders enter our high schools with scores below city and state proficiency levels in math. 64% are below proficiency in reading. 50% of our students speak a language other than English at home.

Urban Observatory

Location: Nationwide

Website: urbanobservatory.org

Richard Saul Wurman, Radical Media, and Esri bring you the Urban Observatory—a live museum with a data pulse.

You'll have access to rich datasets for cities around the world that let you simultaneously view answers to the most important questions impacting today's global cities—and you. Compare and contrast visualized information for a greater understanding of life in the 21st century.

You have the opportunity to join a first-of-its kind virtual experience that takes advantage of GIS as an integrative platform. Information about urbanization does not exist in comparative form. Several cities have already signed on to participate. By contributing, you empower your citizens, constituents, colleagues, and the global community.

The creative and technical forces at Radical Media and Esri build you a one-of-a-kind, futuristic virtual experience that's complete art and science. You'll make your data come to life using an interactive exhibit complete with the finest software, hardware, fiber optics, custom kiosks, quality sound system and monitors.

Urban Prototyping

Location: San Francisco, CA

Website: urbanprototyping.org

UP: San Francisco is a festival centered around Placemaking Through Prototyping: How Citizen Experiments Reimagine the Public Realm. The festival fosters a wide array of new creative projects which blend the digital and physical to explore new possibilities in public space. Every project produced is open source, publicly documented, and replicable in any city in the world.

The project teams behind these works represent exciting new collaborations between the creative technology, participatory art, and urban design communities. The UP Festival series of events – centered around an open call for proposals, a weekend makeathon, and a public street exposition– brought together thousands of participants and attendees, building a community around civic engagement through creative work.

The UP exposition in 2012 served as a high-visibility public venue for showcasing San Francisco's leadership in the fields of technology, design, civic participation, and maker culture.

Urban Retail Institute

Location: Nationwide

Website: urbanretailinstitute.com

The Urban Retail Institute (URI) has been founded to promote sustainable urban retail for historic and new city centers, with the general goal of providing for the goods and services needed and desired by their residents, workers and visitors.

URI offers a platform for learning about new trends, research, history and an industry insider's understanding of all aspects of urban retail planning, development, operations and management. The institute is targeted for architects, concerned citizens, developers, educators, financial institutions, policy makers, retailers, students and urban planners.

A wide range of urban retail topics are reviewed including: architecture, big box retailers, department stores, cinemas, grocery stores, entertainment, lighting, independent stores, leasing, lifestyle centers, new urbanism, malls, merchandising plans, national chains, neighborhood centers, parks, parking, restaurants, streetscape, store planning, resorts, urban planning, visual merchandising and zoning policy.

URI offers educational workshops, white papers, research and peer review for urban retail development and planning.

Urban Strategies Council

Location: Oakland, CA

Website: urbanstrategies.org

The Urban Strategies Council (USC) is a community building support and advocacy organization located in Oakland, California. Founded as a non-profit in 1987, the council works with stakeholders in low-income communities, community-based organizations, and public systems to expand services for children and families, improve health, educational, and other outcomes, and increase employment and economic opportunities

The focus of the USC's work is to support youth, family and community development as a means of building healthy, vibrant communities in order to reduce persistent poverty. The USC is a community building support and advocacy organization. The council's approach to its support work is focused on working community stakeholders to build strategies and capacities (including our own) for effective collective action.

USC recognizes that sustainable change involves not only building strategies and capacities, but also requires the exercise of leadership to build a common agenda for change that will improve outcomes for children and families.

Urban Times

Location: International

Website: urbantimes.org

Welcome to the go to place for optimists and forward-thinkers. This is citizen journalism curated for the people by the people.

We launched Urban Times to tackle the sensationalism and hearsay that permeates the news and media culture of today. Our content is entirely user-generated as citizen journalists and thought-leaders from across the globe submit their content to be edited for free. By mixing the scale and impact of a mega content generator with the positive values and culture of a small startup, we will rewire the global worldview towards solutions-oriented thinking.

Urban Times is the sustainable future of online publishing. Our doors are open to all potential contributors, whether you're a writer, editor, designer, developer or something else entirely: GET INVOLVED!

UrbDeZine

Location: Nationwide

Website: urbdezine.com

UrbDeZine is a 'web-zine' about regional architecture, design, and culture.

Essentially, this site is about the design of your community. Whether that is architecture, urban planning, transportation, historic preservation, ecology, or culture, UrbDezine is designed to provide the fastest and most comprehensive information by being an interactive community forum.

UrbDeZine is for people who are passionate about the design of their community. Submit articles and images to info@urbdezine.com, along with a photo (head shot) and professional biography (limit 5 pgs). Your profile and a link will be included in articles/images selected for publication.

The Author Panel is invitation only but if you are interested in being on the panel, please submit your qualifications. Qualified and committed article submitters may be invited for inclusion on the panel. Article writing for UrbDeZine is an excellent way to influence design for the better, as well as an excellent way for design professionals to market themselves through the web and social media, and improve the SEO of their own websites.

Vancouver Public Space Network

Location: Vancouver, BC

Website: vancouverpublicspace.ca

Vancouver Public Space Network (VPSN) is here to preserve and celebrate public space as an essential part of a vibrant, inclusive city. The VPSN is a grassroots collective that engages in advocacy, outreach and education on public space issues in and around Vancouver, British Columbia.

This includes challenging the increase of advertising 'creep' in public places, promoting creative, community-friendly urban design, monitoring private security activities in the downtown core, fostering public dialogue and democratic debate, and devising creative ways to re-green the neglected corners, alleys and forgotten spaces of the city. We also like to devise ways to have fun in public space.

VPSN was formed in 2006. Since that time our numbers have grown from a dozen initial participants to over 1500 members. The network continues to expand – a testament to the large number of individuals who value public space and view it as an essential feature of a vibrant, inclusive city.

Visual Artillery

Location: International

Website: visualartillery.com

We're Visual Artillery, an international street art collective, and a certified nonprofit organization.

We function as a network for artists, and as an educational service to developing countries and struggling communities to provide them with art, training, and experience.

We're "against" the destruction of property, and we're "for" the empowerment of society through street art, graffiti art, and urban-inspired art.

Walkable and Livable Communities Institute

Location: Nationwide

Website:
https://www.aarp.org/livable-communities/act/walkable-livable-communities/info-12-2012/walkable-and-livable-communities-institute.html

The Walkable and Liveable Community Institute (WLCI) helps to create healthy, connected communities that support active living and that advance opportunities for all people through walkable and bikeable streets, livable cities and better built environments.

Each year, WLCI directly helps as many as 80 communities across North America by providing technical assistance and working alongside them to plot a course toward a more walkable future.

WLCI also develops and broadly disseminates educational materials and tools that are free to the public and that help to advance the walkability movement. Because a picture is worth a thousand words, we produce inspiring photo-visions to help local leaders and residents see for themselves how walkability, bikeability and livability can transform the community.

Walk Bike Transit

Location: Chicago, IL

Website: walkbiketransit.org

Walk Bike Transit (WBT) is a non-partisan political action committee conceived as a means of engaging in political advocacy that is off-limits to 501(c)3 not-for-profit advocacy groups.

As a political organization, our mission is to influence elections and candidates on behalf of active transportation issues. As such, WBT has mobilized voters all across the city to engage and support local candidates on the importance of better biking, walking and transit options.

Our strategic approach has been built around district and ward-specific events organized by WBT and hosted for candidates around elections. These events have provided voters the opportunity to engage with candidates on the importance of bikeable, walkable and transit-friendly communities. In turn, candidates were given the chance to earn support by demonstrating an understanding and commitment to active transportation issues. Perhaps most importantly, WBT events mark the beginning of an ongoing dialogue about ways in which communities and leaders can work together towards a practical vision for transforming transportation options.

Walk Score

Location: Nationwide

Website: walkscore.com

Walk Score's mission is to promote walkable neighborhoods. Walkable neighborhoods are one of the simplest and best solutions for the environment, our health, and our economy.

Our vision is for every property listing to read: Beds: 3 Baths: 2 Walk Score: 84. We want to make it easy for people to evaluate walkability and transportation when choosing where to live.

Walk Score Professional, makes it easy to integrate Walk Score into other websites. We also provide Walk Score data to researchers.

We have multiple patents pending on our scoring and search technologies. We show over 10 million scores every day and over 20,000 sites use Walk Score services. Walk Score has been featured in hundreds of newspaper articles and TV segments.

WalkSF

Location: San Francisco, CA

Website: walksf.org

Since 1998, Walk San Francisco has been San Francisco's only pedestrian advocacy organization. Through smart, targeted advocacy, Walk SF and its members, are improving city streets and neighborhoods and making San Francisco a more livable, walkable city by reclaiming streets as safe, shared public space for everyone to enjoy.

Walk SF is organized into two separate organizations: Walk San Francisco, a 501(c)4, and the Walk San Francisco Foundation, a 501(c)3. The board governs both organizations and ensures that charitable efforts of Walk SF are separate from restricted activities of the Walk SF Foundation.

Everyone walks at some point in their day, but over the past century, pedestrian safety has become an afterthought in most street design. The result? A built environment in San Francisco which makes walking both unsafe and uninviting. Walk SF partners with city agencies, residents, and nonprofits to undo past decisions and prioritize the redesign of the city's most dangerous streets – the six percent of streets where more than 60% of pedestrian crashes occur.

WALK [YOUR CITY]

Location: Nationwide

Website: walkyourcity.org

In 1960, 1:4 citizens took one useful, 10 minute walk each day. Now that number is 1:10. More people live in cities now than ever before. What makes a place more or less walkable is determined by the choices you have to walk somewhere useful as part of your everyday routine. Walkability is becoming a major factor in how we, both citizens and cities, are shaping our future communities.

Take ownership of your streets, improve or share the walkability of your street. Walk [Your City] empowers you to promote walkability in your community by creating, producing and installing pedestrian wayfinding signage. Signage that is consistent communication and organization of navigational cues from our surrounding environment (i.e. directional signage to get around).

Walking builds the local sense of community and helps citizens become more engaged. Our platform helps community groups, schools and nonprofits become neighborhood advocates by making it easy for you to promote walkability.

Welcome Table

Location: New Orleans, LA

Website: nola.gov/city/welcome-table

Welcome Table New Orleans is an initiative of the Mayor's Office focused on race, reconciliation and community. The Welcome Table will bring diverse groups of New Orleanians together to share experiences, share stories, build relationships, listen and learn from each other and finally create and execute projects that will build a better, stronger city.

Welcome Table Groups (diverse groups of no more than 25 people) come together to work through a facilitated process of discussion, relationship building and action. By meeting in safe, civil, secure, structured and facilitated spaces, Welcome Table Groups will be able to work through each phase to build greater understanding of each other and critical issues facing our city.

Groups will meet in various locations throughout four parts of the city: Central City, St. Roch, Algiers and Little Woods. However, any resident of New Orleans will be eligible to participate. Projects that develop from each Welcome Table Group will not be required to take place in the neighborhood in which they are conceived.

Western SOMA Voice

Location: San Francisco, CA

Website: westernsomavoice.org

We are a group of people who live in, work in, or are concerned about the area of San Francisco called Western SOMA. The core of Western SOMA is the area bounded by 6th Street and 13th Street, and Mission Street and Bryant Street.

It is an area of sharp contrasts. In additional to much nightlife and business, commercial and retail, new and old, it is home to several schools, as well as many of San Francisco's historic residential enclave districts. It is an area defined by the diversity of uses that make it up.

According to the 2014 Assessor's report this area is a major revenue generator for the city, lagging only the Financial District and Pacific Heights in 2014. The visible cranes tell the story: there is more development coming on-line. It is the base for many homeless and low-income services, both city and charitable organizations.

Why Don't We Own This?

Location: Detroit, MI

Website: whydontweownthis.com

Why Don't We Own This? (WDWOT) is a service by LOVELAND Technologies that displays every property in a city and provides meaningful lenses to understand property information.

The focus of WDWOT is Detroit, Michigan. We started WDWOT in 2011 to track the Wayne County Foreclosure Auction. Each year our work has grown along with the size and scale of the foreclosure auction and its effect on the City of Detroit, and now we're branching out to provide more year-round property and land use services.

We strive to provide property information in a clean and interactive way that is intuitive to use while increasing the sense of ownership and power a citizen has in their city. Hopefully WDWOT helps prevent the accidental and unnecessary loss of properties to tax foreclosure and auction, and helps connect you with otherwise invisible opportunities for enlightenment, investment, charity, and support.

It's free to look up information and comment on WDWOT.

Willamette River Initiative

Location: Oregon

Website: willametteinitiative.org

Home to two-thirds of the state's population and 75% of its economic output, the Willamette Basin is one of the defining features of Oregon. The Willamette River is an important part of our history and our sense of place, and because the river and its tributaries are located entirely within Oregon's boundaries - its destiny is largely in our hands.

Though its water quality has improved considerably since the 1960s, the Willamette faces an uncertain future. Many parts of the river exceed state standards for bacteria, temperature and mercury, and contamination from toxic pollutants is a growing concern. Important habitats and the species that depend on them have declined significantly.

The population of the Willamette Valley is expected to nearly double by 2050, placing additional pressure on the river and surrounding lands. The purpose of the Willamette River Initiative is to achieve meaningful, measurable improvements in the health of the Willamette River and selected tributaries by 2018 and to create a national model for effective philanthropic involvement in the restoration of large, complex ecological systems.

Women's Community Revitalization Project

Location: Philadelphia, PA

Website: wcrpphila.com

The Women's Community Revitalization Project (WCRP) is committed to social and economic equity for low-income women and their families. We develop housing and neighborhood facilities, provide supportive services, advocate for policy change, and honor leadership, dignity, and justice in our communities.

When you start with women, you are at the core of communities and families. There is power in women working together to make change. WCRP has created a model that works for community development, putting that power to work for low-income women and their families.

WCRP values low-income women and their families and their power to make decisions that improve their lives. We honor leaders in our community, find solutions to any challenge, and bring hope and possibility to the women that we serve. We are the Women's Community Revitalization Project. Together we're building a place for everyone.

Women's Housing and Economic Development Corporation

Location: Bronx, NY

Website: whedco.org

The Women's Housing and Economic Development Corporation (WHEDco) is a community development organization founded on the radically simple idea that all people deserve healthy, vibrant communities.

We build award-winning, sustainable, affordable homes but our work is not over when our buildings are complete. WHEDco believes that to be successful, affordable housing must be anchored in strong communities that residents can be proud of.

WHEDco's mission is to give the South Bronx access to all the resources that create thriving neighborhoods from high-quality early education and after-school programs, to fresh, healthy food, cultural programming, and economic opportunity.

World Urban Forum

Location: International

Website: unhabitat.org/wuf

The World Urban Forum (WUF) is a non-legislative technical forum convened by the United Nations Human Settlements Programme (UN-Habitat), hosted in a different city every two years, to examine the most pressing issues facing the world today in the area of human settlements, including rapid urbanization and its impact on cities, communities, economies, climate change and policies. It is the world's premier conference on cities.

Participants at the Forum include, but are not limited to, national, regional and local governments, non-governmental organizations, community-based organizations, professionals, research institutions and academies, professionals, private sector, development finance institutions, foundations, media and United Nations organizations and other international agencies.

The WUF promotes the strong participation of Habitat Agenda partners and relevant international programmes, funds and agencies, thus ensuring their inclusion in the identification of new issues, the sharing of lessons learned and the exchange of best practices and good policies.

Zócalo Public Square

Location: Nationwide

Website: zocalopublicsquare.org

Zócalo Public Square is a not-for-profit daily idea exchange that blends live events and humanities journalism. We foster healthier, more cohesive communities by tackling important contemporary questions in an accessible, non-partisan, and broad-minded spirit.

Zócalo, a project of the Center for Social Cohesion at Arizona State University and the New America Foundation, is based in Los Angeles and Phoenix, and roams across the country. We explore connection, place, big ideas, and what it means to be a citizen, be it locally, regionally, nationally, or globally. We are committed to welcoming a new, young, and diverse generation to the public square.

Although filled with community activity thanks to its wealth of museums, universities, and specific community organizations, L.A.'s cultural landscape was essentially segregated. Public events were in fact semi-private, targeted by ideology, race, or ethnicity, or promoted to paying members of particular organizations. Zócalo was designed to invigorate and integrate the city's public discourse.

100 en 1 dia Bogotá

Location: Bogotá, Colombia

Website: bogotavisible.com

There's a limit to the amount of physical change one person or a small group of people can initiate in a city, but what if hundreds of citizens united, each putting in place the projects and changes they want to see in their city all on the same day? That's the goal of 100en1día (100 in 1 day) – a social movement originating from Bogotá, Colombia, which aims to inspire citizen driven change on a significant scale, transforming cities over a 24 hour period.

The project has already encouraged hundreds of interventions in the Colombian cities of Bogotá, Pasto, Pamplona and Chinú, with street art, urban gardens and bike lanes all appearing on the same day. Bogotá is currently preparing for their second event and international cities are also beginning to get on board. San José is launching its first event and Cape Town and Copenhagen are running their own versions.

Other cities have already expressed an interest in replicating the project. As a result, the team behind 100en1día are working on developing an online platform to make it as easy as possible to launch local versions.

504ward

Location: New Orleans, LA

Website: 504ward.com

Welcome to 504ward, the home-base for the young talent in New Orleans to meet, learn, explore connect and grow. Allow us to be both your hub and your bridge, your anchor and your sail, your source for deep connection and frivolous nonsense. Our mission? To keep you: the twenty and thirty-somethings living in New Orleans and working to improve it.

Like many others in this city, we are inspired by the influx of talented and motivated young professionals, and we are working to retain these powerful assets by providing access to jobs, leadership, social connectivity, and opportunities of all shapes and colors. This is a powerful moment in New Orleans. While Katrina have been our nation's greatest challenge, it could also be our resounding legacy. For the first time in its storied history, New Orleans is saturated with talented networks of young people, who have followed the road less traveled all the way to the Crescent City.

In what has become an incubator for innovation and intellectualism, New Orleans is watching the development of a generation of leaders, who will pay dividends to their country for generations to come.

596 Acres

Location: New York, NY

Website: 596acres.org

We build online organizing platforms for land access advocates and facilitators. In New York City we are land access advocates and use one of our platforms.

Hundreds of acres of vacant public land are hidden in plain sight behind chain-link fences in New York City, concentrated in neighborhoods disproportionately deprived of beneficial land uses.

We are building the tools for communities to open all these rusty fences and the opportunities within them to improve the areas they live in by making municipal information available online and on the ground (e.g. by placing signs on vacant public land that explain a lot's status and steps that the community can take to be able to use this land, providing education about city government and ways to participate in decisions that shape neighborhoods, assisting communities with legal support and campaign development on land use issues and maintaining a network that allows communities to share knowledge and relationships with decision-makers.

1000 Friends of Oregon

Location: Oregon

Website: friends.org

The passage of Senate Bill 100, which created our innovative land use planning system, was one of Oregon's great bipartisan political achievements.

As historic as that effort was, Governor Tom McCall understood that, to be successful, Oregon needed a citizen watchdog group to ensure that local decisions reflected the voices of Oregonians and not those of special interests. So Governor McCall, along with a young lawyer named Henry Richmond, created 1000 Friends of Oregon. Citizens had a new champion to fight for them.

Since 1975, 1000 Friends of Oregon has defended productive Oregon landscapes and the families they support, while promoting the qualities community, economy and environment that have made Oregon such a special place to live. 1000 Friends has been there every step of the way. We've been doing it for forty years and we'll be at it for at least forty more. No other organization does what we do for Oregon.

Despite the success we have had, there is so much more to do. Oregon must continue to be a leader in "getting it right", striking a balance of productivity, livability and beauty.

colophon:

This book was produced on a Toshiba Chromebook 2.
Google applications such as Docs, Drive, etc.
were used to layout the pages, and format the text.

There are three fonts that were used;

Quattrocento Sans for the text.

Abril Fatface for the page numbers in the body,.

Balthazar for the page numbers in the indexes,

(**Righteous** was used for the main title)

Printing is done by Createspace.
Fulfillment and shipping are through Amazon.

gratitude:

Thank you to my coworkers and planning directors at:
The City of South San Francisco,
the County of San Mateo and
the County of Santa Cruz.